PALO ALT...
LIBR...
PlEASE RETURN

MW00425649

A FLASH OF GREEN

MEMORIES OF WORLD WAR II

CHARLES S. MCCANDLESS

EDITED BY
SANDRA MCCANDLESS SIMONS, PHD

Copyright © 2018 by Charles S. McCandless

All rights reserved. No part of this publication may be reproduced, distributed, or transmitted in any form or by any means, including photocopying, recording, or other electronic or mechanical methods, without the prior written permission of the author, except in the case of brief quotations embodied in critical reviews and certain other noncommercial uses permitted by copyright law.

ISBN: 978-1-64314-603-4 (Paperback)

AuthorsPress Publishing
California, USA
www.authorspress.com

Contents

Charles Sprague McCandless in 1944.

Foreword

I CAN STILL PICTURE MY FATHER SITTING IN OUR LIVING ROOM READING. Nearly every evening, he would settle into our couch and read tome after tome about war, particularly World War II. As a teenager, I wondered why he didn't read books on other topics—or fiction by notable authors. I now understand that he was trying to put himself in the context of the events that occurred around him during his years in the Pacific Theater. My dad was walking to his duty post at Pearl Harbor when he saw the U.S.S. *Arizona* bombed, he was shot down during the Battle of Midway, and he was a frogman at Iwo Jima; but it wasn't until many years later that he understood how these experiences fit into the overall strategies and chain of events in World War II that we read about today. And it wasn't until he wrote this book that any of us in the family even knew about his role in these historic battles.

In 1987, Dad told me that he had written a memoir and asked if I would help him shape it into a book. He gave me a typed manuscript and said he'd like about twenty copies—just enough for family and a few friends.

I was in publishing at the time and started reading the manuscript, red pencil in hand. The book started with my dad's descriptions of his life before the war, and I enjoyed learning about my father as a young man: his first jobs after graduating from college in 1939, his decision to go to Hawaii in the early 1940s, and his first flying lessons. But as these stories led to his wartime experiences, I had a mix of feelings—amazement, surprise, pride—and a deepening sense of just how much his experience in the war shaped him.

We knew that my dad had been at Pearl Harbor. But he rarely spoke of these experiences, even to my mother. We had no idea that he had been a dive bomber pilot at Midway, crashed his plane at Guadalcanal, or served as a Seabee in Ulithi Atoll, Peleliu, and Saipan. We did not know that he was a frogman at Iwo Jima, or struggled to get out of the Philippines after the Japanese surrendered in 1945.

Sometimes, I felt as if I was reading a good war novel; then I would remember that I knew the main character and the action wasn't fiction. For the first time, I had a small window into what it was like for my dad to live through the war.

After reading his memoir, I asked my dad why he ended his story in 1945. He explained that when he finished writing about the war, he had nothing else to say. It was those experiences that profoundly influenced his thinking, shaped the fearlessness with which he started and ran two successful businesses, and solidified his decision to go from being a devoutly religious Christian to an atheist. It was a piece of his life that he had kept largely to himself, and he thought it time to share the experiences that had so greatly affected him with his children and grandchildren.

Thirteen years after his death, I feel it is important to share my dad's stories with a broader audience. This slice of one man's journey provides a glimpse into both our country's history and the realities of war. History books can relay the facts of each battle and analyze the strategic decisions of the leaders at the time, but it is only through the sharing of individuals' unedited stories that we see the texture and detail in the threads that make up that larger tapestry.

It is these personal stories that remind us of the extraordinary things that ordinary men and women do during times of war: they take risks, win struggles, and witness losses that most of us cannot even imagine. While these experiences are often too terrifying to explain to those who weren't there to share them, they are important for all of us to hear. Without these stories, we cannot fully understand or consider the consequences of being at war. Nor can we appreciate the courage, strength, and sacrifice it takes to safeguard the freedom and security that we experience everyday in the U.S.

My dad's memoir fills in a piece of the World War II tapestry that he spent so much time studying. As I read it again, I feel an everlasting sadness that he is no longer here, but I am thankful that he took the time to record his story for his children and grandchildren. It is an engaging and remarkable story—we often joke that my dad had nine lives. But it also provides a first-person perspective on the important events of the war. By publishing it beyond our family, I hope to bring this piece of history alive for those who were not there to live it and inspire others to tell their own stories for future generations.

—*Sandra McCandless Simons*

Navy recruiting poster aimed at recent or soon-to-be college graduates.

ONE

Graduation and the
First Construction Job

S TANFORD UNIVERSITY IS LOCATED ON LAND WHICH was originally a horse farm. It was the summer home of Leland Stanford, whose hobby was raising horses for carriage racing and thoroughbreds. Because Leland Stanford called his country place The Farm, many students and even the newspapers also refer to it as The Farm. President Herbert Hoover, one of Stanford University's first and most prestigious graduates, gave it another name, The Country Club, because it was a small, expensive university in a beautiful country setting and had a golf course, stables, and polo fields.

The forty-eighth annual graduation commencement of the Stanford Country Club was to take place June 18, 1939, in the Greek Amphitheater on campus. I was to be one of about 800 seniors to graduate that year, and it was a large class considering the entire undergraduate school enrollment was less than 3,600.

On Saturday night the week before graduation, I went to the senior ball with a lovely girl named Betty Crawford. I wore a white tuxedo, and she was dressed in a beautiful white formal and wore the orchid corsage I had sent her. We went to dinner at L'Omelette with a gang of friends, drank too much champagne, danced until 2:00 a.m., partied some more at a friend's house in Menlo Park until 4:00 a.m., and then drove up into the hills to watch the sun rise over Mt. Hamilton, still drinking champagne. On Monday morning after the dance, I had to go to work on my first professional job as a construction surveyor. Earl C Thomas, Professor of Highway Engineering at Stanford, had contracted to perform all the surveying for the construction of what is now the Permanente Cement Plant in the hills behind Cupertino. To accomplish this, Thomas hired six of the twenty or so graduating civil engineers to fill out the skeleton crew of more experienced professional surveyors. One of the requirements for getting the job was that we had to start work a week before we formally graduated. Finals were over so there really wasn't a problem. We'd just miss some good parties.

The regular working week was six days. The pay was excellent and we could work overtime. My job was particularly interesting as my party of five was assigned to lay out a mile long conveyor system which would bring new limestone down the mountain from the quarry to the plant.

From where we were working, we could look down on the beautiful Santa Clara Valley—hundreds of acres of neat, green orchards extending from Los Gatos to what is now Fremont, San Jose, and Palo Alto. Most of the little towns, such as Sunnyvale and Campbell, were nearly obscured by the fruit trees. The Diablo Mountain Range stood in the background. When I first started, I carried the lunches and heavy bundles of wooden stakes and was in charge of all other portable paraphernalia. Another one of my jobs, which I later came to regret, was to grub out the poison oak.

This was my first surveying job, and by the time it was over I had pretty well learned the trade. Not all was sweetness and light, however. The party chief was Ike Stage, an old pro who thoroughly disliked college men, especially if he believed they were taking a job away from an unemployed professional surveyor.

When graduation day arrived at the end of my first week of work, the weather was beautiful. My Grandfather and Grandmother McCandless, Grandfather Sprague, and my mother attended the ceremonies. Unfortunately, Grandmother Sprague, who was eighty-five, was in poor health and to her great disappointment and mine was unable to make the trip. With all the pomp and tradition, the graduation ceremonies were impressive, and the day couldn't have been more perfect, with one exception—I had a bad case of poison oak all over my body. I was terribly uncomfortable! However, on the Monday following graduation, I was back on the job, still in charge of portable paraphernalia and still itching.

A couple of weeks later one of the men was transferred, and Stage was forced to promote me to a rear chainman's job. Stage never did stop bitching. He screamed and swore at me the whole time, nicknamed me Bub, and kept complaining about lousy college men and how unlucky he was to have them. Fortunately after six weeks, Stage was transferred. My classmate, Bud Cameron, became chief of party and immediately appointed me his instrument man. From then on everything was fine except that the job terminated at the end of September.

The old Permanente Cement Plant is still operating (1988). Today when I drive between Los Gatos and Sunnyvale, I look up at the mountain behind Cupertino and see the conveyor zigzagging up the hill just as we laid it out forty-nine years ago.

At the end of September, 1939, when the job was over, I loaded my Ford, said good-bye to my friends, and headed for Los Angeles. I had planned to stay home with my mother and grandparents because I hadn't seen them to any extent since I graduated from high school and because my Grandmother Sprague was eighty-five and failing. I had always had a very close relationship with Bidy Sprague and felt that under these circumstances I should stay around for awhile. The family was very pleased to see me and have me stay with them. The first thing I had to do was to get a job. My friend, Henry Layne, a structural engineer from Stanford, had opened his own shop in the Architect's Building near City Hall in downtown Los Angeles, so I went to see him. Sure enough, Layne had engineered the Sears-Roebuck high rise, and Ford Twaits, the contractor who had just obtained the contract to build it, needed a good job engineer.

I applied and got the job. It consisted of all field surveying and layout, checking all dimensions of the work daily, calculating and ordering all materials, developing and keeping track of construction costs, and maintaining "as built" plans plus miscellaneous charts. I loved the job and knew then and there that I'd be a building contractor someday. One thing that made it more attractive than highway construction was that you could live in the city, and I always liked the city better than the country, probably because I was brought up in the city.

The superintendent was a Swede named Oscar Ericson, who was a good boss to work for. One of his dictums was that when I calculated and ordered concrete, sometimes two or three hundred yards, I'd better be right. If I were five yards off, I had to buy him a new hat, which could get expensive since a hat cost five dollars and I only earned a dollar an hour, the same as a carpenter. In eight months, I think I bought him three hats.

Soon after buying Ericson his third hat, I was called into the head office of my boss, Mr. Ford Twaits. He said his company was entering into a joint venture with McDonald-Kahn, Morrison-Knudsen, and some others to build Fort Ord just north of Monterey. The Fort was to accommodate 30,000 men and serve as a major west coast marshaling camp for the purpose of training recruits and forming new army divisions. He offered me a job as staff engineer, which was a considerable promotion since I'd also be chief surveyor for the entire project. This was a chance for me to be involved in the design and layout of streets, sewer, water systems, and drainage for virtually a medium sized city - all from bare land.

It was June 1940, and I had been in Los Angeles eight months. I'd had a good time in L.A. I'd made several friends at work and some old high school friends were still around, including Harry Smith, Bill Bernstein, Frank Gifford, and Jack Dixon. Besides, when you live on the edge of Hollywood, there's no end to the single girls, three of whom I dated regularly, although I can't remember their names. We went to parties, dances, and to the beach almost every weekend. I liked to dance and was a reasonably competent surfer. Furthermore, I'd purchased a beautiful silver-colored, one-year-old Packard convertible, which didn't hurt my social position one bit. I've always had a love affair with flashy cars, and that car was one of the best. I had a lot of fun.

TWO

Fort Ord, Monterey, California

O N JUNE 3,1940, I KISSED MY GIRL FRIENDS AND FAMILY good-bye and loaded my belongings in the silver Packard. The next morning I put the convertible top down and headed for Carmel, California. It was about an eight hour trip along the coastal route, Highway 101. It started out to be a beautiful warm day, but as I approached Salinas the weather began to cool and the sky became overcast. I pulled into a gas station to fuel the car and put the convertible top back up. I remembered that the coast in this part of California fogged over during the summer. It turned out to be a long, foggy summer and an unusually rainy winter. The sun hardly showed itself during the entire eight months of my stay on the Monterey peninsula.

I arrived in Monterey about 4:00 p.m., settled in a hotel, and telephoned the contact I'd been given. It turned out to be James McClary, a Stanford civil engineer who'd graduated a year before me. Since our last names both, started with "McC" and because of the penchant Stanford professors had for seating students according to the alphabet, I sat next to Jim in a number of classes and knew him well.

"Hi, Mac, I've been waiting to hear from you." He said and then invited me to his home for dinner that night, where I met his wife Jane. It turned out that Jim was a nephew and male heir to the Morrisons of the Morrison-

Knudsen Construction Company, the biggest contractor in the United States. Jim was to be Chief Engineer of the new project and I would be in charge of all field surveys. It was to be a fast track job, the construction would be carried out concurrently with the design, which would be only a few steps ahead. I was to report to the job office in Monterey the next day at 0700. My pay was to be $2 per hour for the first eight hours and $3 per hour for all overtime. We were to work forty-eight hours regular time and twelve hours overtime a week - $132 a week. This was a bonanza! A good apartment was $30 a month; a four bedroom house was $50 a month; and the best steak dinner in town was $1.50. I could save $400 a month and live like a king. I surely was in luck.

The next day I reported to work and was asked to figure out how many surveying parties and what equipment I would need initially. Then Jim asked me how long it would take me to make him a topo map of the 1,000-acre property. I studied the matter awhile and told him I'd like to split the property into four areas. Then once we started, I could give him the field data for one area per week, providing I could work seven ten-hour days. He was to have an office crew under my direction plot the field data daily. I could work three six-man crews on a 250-acre area at one time. I didn't think we could go any faster and still be sure the data was accurate because each day's plot had to be rechecked by me, personally, in the field.

Jim gave me a surprised look and said, "Jeeziz Christ, there's no way you can go that fast."

I bet him a steak dinner for four people at any restaurant the winner chose that I could. I didn't have the fourth person for dinner, but I figured I could find a date even though I had no days off. Jim took me up on the bet, and I could see he was pleased because he said, "Mac, you're my kind o' guy!"

I replied, "Thanks, Mac!"

I found my date more easily and sooner than I had expected. In the personnel office I was interviewed and signed up by a cute, freckled, red-haired young lady. I checked her left hand and, seeing no wedding band, confessed to her in a dejected, unassuming way that I was lonely, bored, friendless, and worried about my new job. I asked if she'd have dinner with me that night to add a little cheer to my very dull life.

She looked me straight in the eyes and replied, "I don't believe a word of it. I think you're a wolf, but I can handle wolves. I'll have dinner with you."

I was a little set back by her cosmopolitan reply, but very pleased. Her name was Martha; she was fresh out of Radcliff; and she shared a house in Carmel with a friend. That was about all the dope I had on her, but it was enough.

When I went back to the engineering office across the hall, Jim was smiling and said, "I happened to notice you talking to Martha Twaits. Nice girl, huh? Did you know her in L.A.?"

"No! Is she Ford Twaits' daughter?" I asked. "She sure is, " Jim replied.

Boy, was I in luck. I hit gold twice: a Stanford friend for a boss and the daughter of the big boss for a date. I was going to like this job just fine. From then on things went very well. I moved from my apartment to a four-bedroom furnished house which I shared with three other single engineers from the job. We hired a housekeeper and cook for $4 a day, had most of our meals at home, and worked hard. We were up at 5:30 a.m., to bed about 10:00 p.m., and worked six days a week, sometimes seven. We didn't socialize a great deal because of our schedule, but I managed to go out to dinner once a week with Martha. She went out with other people, but I didn't have much time to look around for any other company.

Carmel was a very small, quiet, picturesque, seaside town populated mainly by retired people, but there were also many weekend cottages. The town was clustered around one main street which sloped from the highway to the beach. The whole area was heavily wooded with Monterey pine and cypress trees and was very beautiful. Nearby were some golf courses, the 17 Mile Drive which was quite new, and Carmel Valley, which was primarily ranch land. The main entertainment spots were a host of tea rooms run by little old ladies and two or three bars that served dinner. If one wanted anything fancier than that, he had to go to the larger town of Monterey. Monterey was a beach community of predominantly one- and two-story wooden buildings with a bleached waterfront look and an industrial district of fish canneries supplied by a sizable fishing fleet. The cannery district also included a large red-light district with all the usual peripheral entertainment and bars. Because of the cannery, the whole town smelled fishy. Monterey did have one very nice place to go—The Del

Monte Hotel. It was a large, first class, expensive hotel located on the edge of town and situated in a beautiful wooded setting. This was generally where we went to dinner on Saturday nights because of its overall quality and a very fine swing dance band.

On October 16, 1940, the United States put into effect the National Selective Service Act, the draft, which required every able-bodied man over eighteen years of age to make himself available for induction into the armed services. By now anyone who read the papers realized that the United States was preparing for war, but this draft really punched the matter home. Things were getting serious! However, before I went to the selective service office in Monterey to sign up, McClary asked me to request a deferment on the premise that I was working in a civilian job vital to the best interest of the United States. Good civil engineers were in short supply and would be even harder to find now that we had a draft. It ended up that Jim, myself, and the other crew members under thirty all received a six-month exemption, which could be renewed as long as we were working on a job that affected the military.

In November my Grandmother Sprague died at the age of eighty-five. I received a telegram the day of her death. I took leave and drove to Los Angeles to console my grandfather and mother and, of course, attend the funeral. We had the service in the chapel at the Hollywood Cemetery, where she was buried in the family plot next to her son, Harold. The Episcopalian service was conducted by the Reverend Hershey from the St. James Cathedral, the family church.

I returned to Monterey a couple of days after the service and found that something new had happened: the first troops had moved into several sections of the partially-completed barracks. One section was "Officer's Country," living quarters for officers only. It turned out that the officers were the activated Reserve Officers Training Corps graduates from west coast colleges, including Stanford. I went over to the barracks to see if I could find anybody I knew. When I got there, I found that all the officers were second lieutenants and were dressed in World War I outfits—Sam Brown belts, riding breeches, and boots with spurs.

The Stanford contingent were almost all members of the horse-drawn field artillery, while a few were ordinance officers. At Stanford the

R.O.T.C. had been popular with students who were horsemen because they could use army horses stationed on campus as polo ponies. The problem now was that there were no horses for any purpose. It also became apparent that the Army had paid no attention to their reserves during peace time, since about 200 second lieutenants varied in age from 21 to 50. In the years between graduation and mobilization, no training had been made available; thus no promotions were made. I found out later that the horsemen were all ordered to Fort Bragg and turned into tankers and heard that there were more tank commanders from Stanford in Patton's third Army than from any other university - including West Point. I don't know if this is true or not, but my friend Bob Fullerton, a tank commander in the third Army who came home without a leg, said it probably was.

When Christmas, 1940, came around, I decided to take a week off and spend the time with my Grandfather and Grandmother McCandless. They were living in a construction camp at Keen, California, a tiny community located between Bakersfield and Tehachapi, where Dad (Grandfather McCandless) was superintendent of a highway reconstruction project. I drove down in the rain. When I arrived, I gave Bidy Mac a box of candy and Dad a box of cigars. On Christmas, we again exchanged gifts and had a good time.

As usual, I was very careful not to antagonize Dad in any way because of his bad temper; so all we talked about was construction. Since he was an expert with explosives, he was always assigned jobs which involved heavy blasting and cutting and filling with power shovels and trucks. Consequently, he was very interested in my job, where this type of equipment had been replaced with huge self-powered caterpillar scrapers called carry-alls. Of course, we were working on relatively flat land and rolling dunes, not mountainous terrain. After that visit, I was not to see my grandparents again until November, 1942.

By February of 1941, I had been on the project for over eight months, and the initial job was almost completed. In fact, the major surveying work was completed, and I was working in the office designing underground pipeline systems for a second military job. I was getting restless and bored. Even fast promotion and pay raises didn't carry the old-time psychological lifts. What had once been exciting was now dull city. It was time to move on.

The beach at Waikiki, with the Moana Hotel in the background, circa 1940.

THREE

Hawaii

BECAUSE I HAD ALWAYS WORKED DURING MY COLLEGE vacations, I hadn't had a real vacation for five or six years. I decided that I would use the $2,500 that I had saved to take a long vacation. I would then join one of the armed services, since I would be drafted sooner or later. I discussed my plan with Martha over dinner at the Del Monte Hotel one evening, and she thought it was a good idea. She agreed that I should go some exotic place before I was drafted and then look over the various military programs and volunteer for the one of my choice. She even suggested that before I quit my job, I renew my six-months draft exemption to be sure of six months free. I thought about going to Europe, but they were all at war there.

It was then that Martha came up with the idea of going to Hawaii. "I'm going to Hawaii for a month," she said. "Why don't you go over at the same time, and we can date while I'm there?"

We agreed to both book passage on the *Lurline* for the March 7 departure. She would go first class; and I, in cabin class to save money. The price for me was $85 one way, about half the cost of first class. What I didn't know then was that cabin class was completely sealed off from first class and that there was considerable difference in the amenities between the classes. In first class they dressed for dinner (tuxedoes and formals), danced, had more elaborate food, and much nicer cabins—not that cabin class on the Lurline wasn't nice. It was.

I gave the company notice that I was leaving March 1, sold the Packard to one of the engineers, and took a bus to San Francisco on the night of February 28. I stayed there three or four days with a friend, then took a coastal steamer to San Pedro, where I transferred to the pride of the Matson Steamship Line, the luxury-liner Lurline.

There were 250 passengers booked in cabin class and probably 750 in first class. The first class passengers had use of the forward three-quarters of the ship and all four promenade decks. The cabin class passengers had use of the aft one-quarter of the ship and two decks: the main deck, including the fan tail, and a second platform deck above it. The outside passages leading forward from the cabin class areas to first class were barricaded by metal mesh fences. The inside passages were secured by locked doors. There was no apparent way first and cabin class passengers could mix. This arrangement seemed to completely thwart the plans Martha and I had made to see each other. Had I discovered this situation before I purchased the ticket, of course I would have gone first class. The fact that there were two classes should have alerted me to the situation, but it didn't.

Fortunately I had made arrangements to get in touch with Martha when we were all aboard. We shoved off from Los Angeles Harbor about 5:00 p.m. I went to my cabin, sat on the bed, and read all the literature I found on the bureau concerning the Lurline. The booklet contained instructions for use of the ship's facilities in both classes. It described the amenities, rules and regulations, safety drills, specified a dress code, and definitely warned passengers to stay only in the spaces assigned to them. The dress code in first class required tuxedoes to be worn after 6:00 p.m. in the saloons, which included cocktail lounges and dining rooms. The booklet also included a detailed map of the ship.

As I studied the map, I noticed that the first class and cabin class had connecting kitchens. Then I got to thinking: What would happen if a cabin-class passenger wearing a tuxedo walked into the kitchen after dinner? Wouldn't he be asked to go back to first class? Also, after the dancing was over at 12:30 a.m., there was a midnight supper. It followed then, that there must be a small kitchen crew working very late, or maybe all night, and that very possibly a tipsy passenger not wearing a tuxedo, walking into the kitchen at 1:00 a.m. looking for the rest rooms, would be requested to go back to the cabin class area. The trick was not to let the entry into the kitchen be observed, to be sure to have some money in my pocket in case some cook did see me and decided to call the concierge, and to carry a suit bag. The next problem was finding a way to contact Martha.

Just then there was a knock on the door. It was a cabin boy with a message from Martha. She had discovered the same problem. The note instructed me to meet her at the separating fence in the left-hand corridor on the main deck at 6:30 p.m.—in fifteen minutes. I immediately took off for the main deck and headed up the left hand side of the ship. Sure enough, there was Martha coming to meet me. Talking to her through the fence made me think of visitor's day in a jail as depicted in the movies. After an excited greeting and an attempted kiss through the fence, I explained my plan. "It sounds like Cinderella in reverse," she said. She then proceeded to solve the clothes exchange problem by suggesting that we could pass the clothes on hangers through a slit in the side of the fence, right where we were standing. Assuming I managed to get into first class, I could change clothes in her cabin. One thing was paramount. We had to eat dinner at our respective assigned tables and seats because if the waiter discovered a vacant seat, the ship was searched until the missing passenger was located. This procedure assured the captain that no one had disappeared overboard. We also agreed that we should see that our dinner hour was the second seating. We chose this time because after the second seating, confusion would reign while the last diners departed and the tables were cleared from the dance floor. My hours in first class would be from 9:00 p.m. to 1:00 a.m. This way we could dance and partake of the midnight supper for four consecutive nights, providing of course, that all went well.

The plan worked better than we ever hoped. The first night at 9:00 p.m. when I walked into the kitchen with a cocktail glass in my hand, wearing a black tux with a gardenia in the lapel, nobody paid attention. Finally, a head cook spotted me and came over. I smiled and told him that I was a little seasick and disoriented and that I was trying to find a restroom. He very politely showed me the door to first class and gave me directions to the rest room. I then trotted between the waiters moving tables and into the bar, where Martha, looking like a queen in a white formal, was waiting for me.

That evening we danced, drank champagne, and ate at the midnight buffet. She gave me her state room key and directions to her cabin. I changed into a sport coat, left the tuxedo on the bed, and headed for the kitchen door. When I entered the kitchen, practically the same thing as before happened.

The head cook, a different one, came over to me. I smiled, and said that I was drunk and disoriented and was trying to get back to my cabin. He politely guided me to the cabin class door.

The next night I repeated the performance, but this time the head cook recognized me and immediately knew what was going on. I explained the situation truthfully, gave them each ten dollars, which was a whole day's wages, and they managed to ignore me for the rest of the trip. One cook told me that if I should be caught by a head waiter, I could probably make the same arrangement.

The trip was beautiful and smooth, one of the most memorable voyages I've made. The band was great and played currently popular swing, dreamy ballads, and well-known Hawaiian songs. During the midnight suppers we had a hula floor show, the first I'd ever seen.

As we approached the islands the weather got warmer, the sunsets more tropical, and sea life more numerous. First, the flying fish appeared and schools of dolphin accompanied the ship; then the phosphorescent foam appeared in the ship's wake. Finally, on the fourth day, in the distance appeared Kauai, then Oahu, then Molokai, all with billowing clouds covering their volcanic peaks. For me, it was love at first sight.

We approached Oahu Island from the west. The great ship swung down Kauai Channel just outside the reef, passed Makapuu Head, Koko Head, and Diamond Head, and sailed into Mamala Bay. First we passed Kapiolani Park with its polo field, then Waikiki Beach with its three hotels—the large white Moana, next to the pink Royal Hawaiian, and a little beyond the low Halekulani—then Fort DeRussy, the yacht basin, and a long green strip that was Ala Moana Park. Finally we took a swinging right hand turn into Honolulu Harbor Channel, at the end of which stood Aloha Tower. In front of us the city clustered around Fort Street and Nuuanu Avenue. It had the ant-heap look of all downtown cities.

But what a setting! Behind the ant heap, climbing the shoulders of the mountains, were the profuse multicolored houses of the suburbs with their windows glinting; and above them, the solid, unchanging mountains stood, their tropic greenness dripping down the valleys and ravines in among the houses. Crowning the mountains were the ever-present billowing white clouds, hiding the mountain peaks and framed by the blue sky behind. From the ship one got that expansive, far-vista look that one gets only on the sea or from a mountain top. There was no truer picture of Honolulu.

As the ship slowly maneuvered alongside Aloha Tower, a band began to play Hawaiian music, beginning with "Aloha." Suddenly, dark skinned girls and men dressed in colorful Hawaiian costumes appeared on deck. The girls began kissing the passengers and placing flower leis around their necks, while the men passed out trays of mai-tais with large pieces of fresh pineapple on little sticks.

The McCandless Building, Honolulu, Hawaii, circa 1920s. Originally built by in 1906 by the McCandless brothers to serve as an office building. It is still used as an office building today.

FOUR

Sunny Jim McCandless

I WALKED DOWN THE GANG PLANK, INTENT ON FINDING the baggage pick-up station, and pushed through a milling crowd of shouting, waving people. The ship would forward baggage to any destination requested. Since I didn't have a hotel yet, I just decided to ask the baggage department to hold my luggage until otherwise notified. I was carrying the personal effects I needed for the first couple of days. When I went to the baggage window, I caught the eye of a dark little man who looked Filipino and was dressed as a chauffeur. As soon as he saw me, he asked if I were Sprague McCandless.

It turned out that he was the chauffeur for Sunny Jim McCandless, who was waiting for me in his car. I had known that my Grandfather McCandless was a relative, friend, and correspondent of James McCandless, who lived in Honolulu, but I didn't know that he had written ahead and told him that I was coming. It was a pleasant surprise. The chauffeur lead me to a black Lincoln in which sat James McCandless. He was a medium-sized, stocky, grey-haired man in his late seventies. He looked like he could be my grandfather's brother. He greeted me with both enthusiasm and cordiality. After the chauffeur arranged for my baggage to be delivered, we took off for the McCandless residence, a large estate in Maunalani Heights which was a beautiful, exclusive residential area located on the mountain behind Diamond Head. The estate overlooked Diamond Head, Waikiki, and most of West Honolulu. The scene was breathtaking.

James lived alone except for his staff—the chauffeur, a cook, housekeeper, maids, and a number of gardeners. The estate covered about twenty acres of land, terraced and landscaped with lawns, native trees, and large beds of exotic flowers. In the middle of the estate, which gently sloped down the mountain toward the ocean, sat the main house surrounded by little houses for the hired help and their families and stables that had been converted to garages.

The residence was three stories. On the first floor were several living and game rooms, a library, a trophy room, a large dining room, and a kitchen. The second floor contained a number of bedrooms and bathrooms, and the third story was a ballroom and bar. The house was furnished with beautiful antique furniture, paintings, trophies, family pictures, and ancient native Hawaiian artifacts including feathered head dresses and costumes, enormous surf boards, tapa cloth, and spears. It was a small museum.

That evening at dinner, James began telling me about his wife and family, and we continued this talk for most of the time I spent as his guest. He and my grandfather were some kind of cousins. James and his two brothers, Lincoln and John, had come from Pennsylvania to the Islands in the late 1880s, when they were young men. They came to Hawaii principally to drill water wells and build irrigation systems for pineapple and sugar cane plantations.

At that time Hawaii was a native kingdom. The reigning queen was Liliuokalani. In 1893 she was deposed by white residents who set up a republic. The McCandlesses were involved in the revolution and served in the legislature until 1898, when the Islands were annexed to the United States as a territory. Over the years the three brothers prospered, married, and accumulated ranches, plantations and other business interests. During the 1920s Lincoln served as the Hawaiian delegate to the United States Congress. Lincoln and John died during the 1930s, but Lincoln's widow was alive and well and resided on an estate similar to Sunny Jim's.

James' stories were fascinating. Not only did he tell of his family and

James "Sunny Jim" McCandless
(1855—1943)

the history of Hawaii, in which the McCandlesses had been very much involved, but he also introduced me to the culture and folk lore of the native Hawaiians. He took me on sight-seeing excursions to the Iolani Palace and several museums including the Bishop and the Queen Emma. We drove over the valley, down to the Blow Hole, and around the island. He played recordings of authentic Hawaiian music, which is quite different from the contemporary version. He showed me tons of family photographs, explained his collection of native artifacts, and described the great parties held in his big ballroom in the old days.

He confided to me that he really didn't need so many servants and gardeners; however, they had worked for him for thirty-five or forty years, living on the property with their families, and were now friends. He felt that he owed them a retirement.

On Saturday he invited me to go to the McCandless Office Building, located by the Aloha Tower, where he said he had business that needed attention. The office building was three stories and constructed of brown lava. It was headquarters for all the family operations. "McCandless Building, 1906" was engraved above the street entrance. We went up to the second floor where Jim had an office with roll-top desks and electric lights with green reflectors hanging from the ceiling on wires. I'm sure nothing had changed in that office since 1906.

When we arrived there were several little old Hawaiian women, dressed in muumuus with the usual flower lei around their necks, waiting on a bench outside his door. He went over to his desk, unlocked a drawer, and withdrew a handful of twenty dollar bills. He gave one bill to each woman. They smiled, thanked him, and left.

"These are friends from my younger days, before I was married—very old friends. They come to see me every Saturday morning," he said with a smile. I guess he owed them retirement like his other employees. I had been with James for four days and felt that I should not impose upon his hospitality much longer. He had his chauffeur drive me over to the Makiki Hotel on Piikoi Street, which he said was an excellent, reasonably-priced, garden hotel. Sure enough, it was great. Each accommodation was a separate cottage in a beautiful garden. The hotel ran an excellent kitchen, and the dining room had a marvelous view of the city. I arranged for a cottage for about forty dollars a month, including breakfast and dinner. This was not cheap in those days, but it was something I could afford. The next day I gave Jim a box of his favorite cigars and moved to the Makiki Hotel. After that, I visited Jim frequently, and we maintained a warm relationship until I left Hawaii in 1942. He died sometime in 1943.

I only saw Martha a few times during her stay in Hawaii. She was the guest of an Army officer and his family, who were stationed and living at Schofield Barracks, the principle U.S. Army post in the central Pacific. Her hosts managed to see that she was flooded with invitations and dates with second lieutenants; and since Schofield was thirty five miles from Honolulu and I didn't have a car, seeing her was very inconvenient. I didn't much care anyway because I had so much to do.

In 1941, Honolulu must have been one of the most beautiful cities in the world. It wasn't the tourist trap it is today. The city is built on the southern slope of the Koolau Volcanic Mountain Range, which rises over 3000 feet from sea level and has a narrow seventeen mile long coastal plain at its foot. The mountains are cut by four beautiful sloping valleys: Manoa, Nuuanu, Palolo and Kalihi. In these valleys most of the better residential areas were situated. The coastal plain was devoted mostly to civic, commercial, industrial, and military installations, except for the recreational beach areas of Kapiolani Park, Waikiki, the Yacht Harbor, and Moana Park. Hawaii is subtropical rather than tropical, even though it is located south of the Tropic of Cancer at 21 degrees north latitude. The constant northeast trade winds bring considerable rainfall, moderate the average daytime temperature to 80 degrees—70 degrees at night—and aid in maintaining a low humidity. The result of this mild climate is a salubrious flora. The entire area from the mountain tops to the seashore is heavily covered with exotic ferns, trees, plants, and flowers.

Ginger, carnations, gardenias, piikake, night blooming ceruse, bird of paradise, several varieties of orchids, and many others species of flower grew in the garden around my living quarters at the Makiki Hotel. Equally beautiful were the many types of tropical ferns and the trees: coconut palms, monkey pod, koa, banyan, flame, papaya, mango, and cassius. The climate also had a very pronounced effect upon the population. In 1941, the population was 200,000. The city seemed uncrowded and the residents led an unhurried, laid-back life. The typical businessman wore light-weight slacks with a loose fitting, short sleeved, colorful Aloha shirt, frequently adorned with a lei of flowers. Women wore muumuus, long, loose-fitting, brightly colored and patterned garments , adorned with lei. Lei could be purchased on most downtown street corners from Hawaiian women sitting on the sidewalk. A ginger, carnation or piikake lei cost ten cents; a gardenia one, fifteen cents; and an orchid lei, twenty-five cents.

There were four good hotels in Honolulu: a multi-storied downtown businessman's hotel called the Alexander Young and three lavish tourist resorts on the beach at Waikiki—the Royal Hawaiian, the Moana, and the Halekulani Hotel. The Royal Hawaiian was a six-story pink building sitting at the best location on the beach. It had dancing nightly, a good dining room and floor show, and the most beautiful cocktail lounge in Honolulu. The Moana was a smaller hotel with a three-sided patio and cocktail lounge open to the sea and a huge banyan tree over on the side. The Halekulani was a small, luxury hotel. Both latter resorts had dining and entertainment, but not on the elaborate scale of the Royal Hawaiian.

The favorite watering spots for the young crowd were Lau Ye Chai's and Trader Vic's. They were popular because they were much more lively and affordable than the hotels. Lau Ye Chai's had the best dance band in Honolulu, and Trader Vic's had the best cocktails and Chinese food.

Besides the hotels and restaurants, recreation facilities were plentiful. Waikiki beach was superb. It was a mile and a half long with little on it except for the three hotels; Fort DeRussy, which was a cluster of one story cabins built in a beautiful park-like setting one-fourth mile west of the Royal; and the private Outrigger Canoe Club. Everything else was a public park.

There were no high-rise apartments or buildings anywhere near Waikiki. Across Kalakaua Avenue from the hotels and in front of the Ala Wai Canal there was only a row of single story shops and the Waikiki Theater.

Depending on circumstances, surfing could be good at Waikiki for both beginners and experienced surfers. There were many even better swimming beaches and private coves for picnics around the island, the most notable of which was the Blow Hole. The beach north of Oahu, which is hit directly by the northeast trade winds, has big breakers, but only very advanced or professional surfers dared to venture out. I swam there a few times, but it was usually too rough. Besides, the water was full of floating Man-of-Wars, jellyfish that really sting when wrapped around a swimmer's neck, arm or leg.

FIVE

Joining the Navy

G ETTING SETTLED IN THE MAKIKI HOTEL WAS EASY. I had relatively little baggage: a footlocker full of clothes that were too warm to wear in Hawaii, a small battery-powered portable radio which was good for the beach, a wind-up phonograph, and about fifty popular records. I belonged to the jazz-swing music cult of the 1930s. Anywhere I went I had music playing and I haven't changed. I still enjoy listening to the old jazz and swing dance bands. My furnished cottage-apartment was excellent. It had a bedroom with connecting bath, a large living room, and kitchenette. I didn't use the kitchenette much except to make coffee or canapes and drinks when I had parties. Daily room service was included in the rent and I only had to walk about fifty yards to the dining room. The whole cottage was enveloped in purple bougainvillea and surrounded by beds of beautiful tropical flowers and monkey pod, kao, mango, and papaya trees. It was truly a Garden of Eden. The food was also very good. It was here I tasted my first mango and papaya, which was served every morning for breakfast along with pineapple and passion fruit juice, as well as the standard American breakfast fare. Dinner consisted of an appetizer, soup, salad, a fish course, entree and dessert. Before coming to Hawaii, the only fish I had really been exposed to was trout. At the Makiki I learned the delights of mahi mahi (dolphin fish), ono (wahoo), aku (tuna), and many others. I especially enjoyed Japanese sashimi, a raw fish which often was offered as an appetizer. Since the Makiki was a Japanese-owned and operated hotel, dinner menus often included Japanese entrees. I'd never encountered such food before. Although at first was a little apprehensive, I was soon enjoying sukiyaki, tempura, sushi, and teriyaki.

At dinner one evening I met Steve Towne and Larry Glosten, both residents of the Makiki. They were about my age and both were naval architects who had joined the Navy Construction Corps as regulars after graduating from the Massachusetts Institute of Technology. Both had been assigned ship construction and repair duties at Pearl Harbor Naval Ship Yard. We soon got to be good friends. I, of course, told them I was on a long-term vacation, planned to join one of the services, and leaned toward the Marine Corps Aviation. They howled about "leathernecks" and insisted I do nothing until I talked to Lieutenant (jg) Jim Robison, USN (United States Navy), a local recruiting officer who had lived at the Makiki until recently marrying. Steve and Larry said that I would meet Robison at the cocktail party they were having the next Saturday night.

The party was a week away, and I didn't want to wait that long to meet Robison. The Monterey Draft Board had already notified the Honolulu Draft Board, and I wasn't sure that they couldn't, and wouldn't, cancel my deferral. I knew they would be hot on my trail, so I asked Larry to introduce me to Robison by telephone, which he did. Jim was very nice and told me that I had many options and that I should meet with him the following morning at the recruiting office on Beretania Street in downtown Honolulu.

Jim Robison was a graduate of the United States Naval Academy, class of 1938, and the son of Admiral S. S. Robison, Chief of the Bureau of Navigation, U.S. Navy. Among the admiral's many responsibilities were: all recruiting, operating the Naval Academy, handling the Naval Reserve, and commissioning new officers. Jim was slated to be an engineering officer on a destroyer, but was temporarily assigned recruiting duties while awaiting his ship's docking Pearl Harbor.

I appeared at the naval recruiting office at 8:30 a.m. sharp. I was met by a short, fat, elderly chief petty officer dressed in a white uniform that had black hash marks the length of his arm signifying years of service. I was greatly impressed; to me he looked like a high ranking officer. He said that Lieutenant Robison wasn't in yet, but he would be right along. He asked if I would join him in having a cup of coffee while I waited. That was my introduction to navy coffee—black, bitter, and so strong you could cut it with a knife. I managed to finish the coffee by the time Jim arrived. He was dressed in an immaculate white uniform—the one with a high collar, gold buttons, and black and gold epaulettes. Now I was really impressed!

He motioned me into the back office, ordered the chief to bring more coffee, and offered me a seat. He said the Navy and Marines needed young men from every civilian occupation as well as eighteen-year-old recruits. All the reserves were now on active duty, and there were still billets for a least 5,000 officers and 50,000 men. Officers had to be college graduates. Medical doctors, civil engineers, CPAs, dentists, architects, and many other specialists. could get direct commissions, which took only three months because they would basically be practicing their civilian profession in the Navy. Other graduates could join a cadet corp as enlisted men and after four or five months, if qualified, could be commissioned as ensigns or second lieutenants for seagoing service. Aviators, which were needed badly and immediately, were required to have three months preliminary training as seaman second class and normally about seven months training as aviation cadets. However, it was taking considerably longer than this since Pensacola was the only existing primary training school and was set up to satisfy only the relatively small peacetime requirements. The lack of training facilities was causing a bottleneck in the production of naval aviators.

Pilots from both the Navy and Marine Corps were qualified as naval aviators and had identical training up to the time they became commissioned and received their wings. Both types had to be proficient in landing on aircraft carriers, but their eventual missions differed. Navy pilots were either assigned to aircraft carrier squadrons or long range patrolling in multi-engine seaplanes, while Marine pilots were land-based and, among other things, trained for close air support of infantry. Both branches of the service had fighters and dive-type bombers, but the Navy also had torpedo planes and multi-engine seaplanes. It was true that Congress had given the Navy approval to greatly expand their training facilities at Jacksonville, Florida, and Corpus Christi, Texas, but these facilities weren't scheduled for completion until 1942.

I had my choice: I could either take a direct commission in the Civil Engineer Corps and be commissioned in about three months, or take a year or more and become commissioned as a naval aviator. It seemed to me that maybe I had better take a direct civil engineer commission and get on with it. I was ruminating over this when Robison said something else. "Too bad you're not already a commercial pilot! The Navy grabs them up fast"

"Do they have to go to Pensacola?" I asked.

"I don't know the details," he answered.

I invited him to lunch at Trader Vic's, where neither of us had been, and he readily accepted. It was only 11:30 a.m., and Jim wanted to complete some rush paper work. I went out to the front room to borrow a phone book from the chief, made a reservation at Trader Vic's, and then turned to the aviation headings in the yellow pages. There it was, "Myrna Kelly Flight School," located on the other side of the island. I hastily wrote down the phone number for future reference. Jim knew where Trader Vic's was, so we took his Navy car. Vic's was a small building located on Kalakaua Ave. on the way to Waikiki. Inside, it was full of bamboo furniture, fishing nets with blue glass floats hanging on the ceiling, and potted tropical plants and palm trees. There were native waitresses with sarongs draped well above their knees—just like the south sea islands looked in the movies—and, of course, Hawaiian background music. On the floor among the foliage was a real outrigger canoe. I loved it!

We ordered Mai Tais, and I excused myself to make an important phone call. I stopped at the bar to get a hand full of change, found a pay phone, and dialed the number for Myrna Kelly's Flight School. When what I thought to be a man answered, I said, "I'd like to speak to Myrna Kelly, please." The voice replied, "This is she."

"My name's Charles McCandless and I don't know how to fly. How long will it take to get a commercial license?" I asked. "As fast as you can accumulate 200 hours," she answered. "I need it in ten weeks or sooner," I explained.

To which she responded, "If you have the time, I have."

"How much will it cost?" was my next question.

"Five dollars an hour for the plane, and five dollars for the instructor—that includes gas. Ground school's free. You'll need about fifty hours dual." I quickly figured that was $1,250, which was no problem. I had over $3,000 in the bank. "Can I start tomorrow?'"

"Sure! See you at 9:00 o'clock tomorrow morning," Myrna replied. I went back to Jim and the Mai Tais. "Can you find out the requirements for joining the Navy using the commercial pilot route? I'm a commercial pilot." I said.

He looked astounded, then disbelievingly. asked, "Why in hell didn't you tell me that before?"

"You didn't tell me about it until the end of our interview, after I'd already talked myself into going the civil engineering route," I explained.

"Okay, I'll find out. You may have to go to the mainland, but I feel sure they can check you out here." Jim said.

"How about getting the civil engineer commission first—as a back up in case I don't pass? Then if I do pass, I'll transfer," I suggested.

"That's a good idea," Jim replied, "but hard to do. It means a transfer from staff to line. However, there's one good thing about being commissioned when you make the transfer. You're sure to get a commission in the line. They're not likely to reduce your rank to a flying chief or something else, but let's apply for the CEC commission today."

It was March 14, 1941. Applying for the CEC commission entailed filling out endless papers and sending them to the Navy Department. I would have to arrange to supply my birth certificate, college transcript, a copy of my diploma, three letters of recommendation from prominent citizens, and a letter of recommendation from the President of Stanford University.

A Beechcraft Model 17 Staggerwing biplane, similar to the one the author learned to fly with Myrna, his flight instructor.

SIX

Myrna and Flight School

THE NEXT DAY I RENTED A CAR AND DROVE OVER the Pali (mountain pass) to take my first flying lesson. Myrna Kelly, who owned the flight school, would be my personal teacher. She was short and husky, rough and tough, and fairly foul mouthed—a diamond in the rough. In reflecting on the various aviation instructors I have flown with during my life, I believe Myrna was one of the best. Other flyers have told me that one's first instructor is always the best, so maybe that is it.

Myrna employed one full-time and several part-time instructors and owned several small Piper Cubs, a Fleet biplane, and a WACO Scout, which was bigger and heavier than the Fleet. She also had access to a beautiful five-place Staggerwing Beech biplane furnished with a 450 hp Wasp Junior engine, which she generally used for charters. She said I should use the Fleet because it was virtually the same plane as the N3N used by the Navy for primary and basic flight instruction. Later I would fly in the WACO and finish with the Beech, which was approximately the size of the Navy SNJ-2 which has a 550 hp Pratt and Whitney Wasp engine and was used by the Navy for advanced instruction.

As soon as I walked into the office Myrna asked me about my education. Having been a surveyor and map-maker would make navigation a snap and the engineering courses I had taken at Stanford, Principles of Aerodynamics and Design of Airplane Structures gave me more theory than I would have gotten at Pensacola.

"Most of these Navy pilots don't know why a plane flies," Myrna said. (I learned later that this wasn't true.) "Do you get scared or air-sick?"

"No, I don't think so. At least I never have before," I replied.

Before I got aboard the Fleet, Myrna gave me instructions, "Keep your hands off the controls, feet flat on the floor, your hands in your lap or on the cowling. If you puke, do it over the side and not in the cockpit, 'cause you're gonna clean it up. If you crap in your pants, raise your right hand and I'll land. Don't watch the instruments, watch the horizon. Always watch the horizon!"

Then she handed me a leather jacket, a parachute and leather helmet with goggles and said, "Let's go!" She helped me get the parachute on, showed me how it worked, and then told me to "get my ass" in the front seat of the Fleet.

When I climbed in that plane, the memories and romance of those books and movies about World War I aviation which I devoured as a kid all came floating back—*War Birds, Wings, Hell's Angels, Dawn Patrol, The Red Baron*. Frankly, over the years my feelings haven't changed much. I still look at the sky when I hear an engine overhead and enjoy hanging around the old planes at the airport. Even when Myrna started the engine, it was just like the movies—switch on, contact, switch off, as the wooden prop was pulled around until the engine caught.

We were off! The plane climbed like a balloon. When Myrna finally leveled off, she spoke through the speaking tube, "This is straight and level. Look at the horizon and the wing tips and keep watching it while I turn." We turned left, turned right, ascended, descended, did circles and figure eights. Then she asked, "How ya doin'?" "Never had it so good!" I returned.

"Okay, here we go. This is a loop. Watch the horizon. How ya doin?" she asked again.

I answered, "Let's go!"

Whap! We did a snap roll left, then a snap roll right, then an Immelmann. "Okay, here's a real test—a spin," she said.

I was feeling queasy, but I wasn't telling her! Suddenly, I was looking straight down and the world was cartwheeling. I never thought it would stop. I was now definitely getting queasy. The plane pulled out and climbed again like a balloon; then suddenly the whole thing happened again, only in the other direction.

"Did you puke?" she asked.

"No!"

"Are you scared? Do you want to land?" she queried.

"Hell no!" I said. The fact was I did because my stomach was churning. I was secretly relieved when she replied, "We're going to land anyway!"

Myrna made a beautiful dead stick, three-point landing, taxied to parking, and shut the engine down. We climbed out. "You did very well, Mac," she said. "Now we can get on with it. See you at 1:00 p.m. in the office. You can get something to eat at the snack bar."

After lunch Myrna and I made our plans. I would fly three days a week, seven hours a day for ten weeks. She was empowered to issue both the private and the commercial license. All I needed to get started was a physical exam which she said I could take care of any time in the next few weeks. Myrna said she could develop my flying skills through the equivalent of the Navy advanced course except for things the Navy wouldn't expect a civilian commercial pilot to know such as gunnery, formation flying, radio communications, tactics, and navy regulations. We agreed that I would teach myself ground school and how to communicate in telegraphy to a speed of at least twenty four words per minute with a key, which was required of all commercial and naval pilots. Since I was already adequately trained in navigation, including some celestial and some aerodynamics, ground school should be no problem at all. Myrna would even loan me a copy of the current *Naval Aviator's Training Manual* as well as other training books. Everything looked good!

After the afternoon lesson which focused on airplane pre-flight checks, engine starting procedures including hand-cranking the prop, ground and flight safety procedures, aircraft instrumentation, and fuel management, we quit for the day. It was late in the afternoon, so I called a cab and went home. I spent the evening calling newspaper ads, looking for a used cars. The next day I bought a year-old Ford convertible for $500. I also purchased, by mail order, the flying gear I would need: a fur-lined leather jacket, head gear, and goggles. That same day I had my first real lesson. Myrna advised me that regardless of what I'd heard about soloing in eight hours, I had better figure ten hours. She automatically added on two hours of tail spins and—did she! Before she turned me loose, I entered spins from every possible angle until I could come out on any given heading. It was an exciting and eventful week, ending with Steve and Larry's cocktail party on Saturday night. They got me a blind date from somewhere. Robison and his wife, plus some other couples, mostly unmarried, attended. I don't know why the hotel didn't call the police. Except for me, it was an all-navy crowd that didn't stop yelling and drinking until 3:00 a.m. The party started formally with Hawaiian rum punch, but by midnight it was booze straight from the bottle with everybody doing their version of the hula, sometimes on a table.

Before the party got going, Robison told me that I could make my appointments with the Navy to take the flight test at Pearl Harbor Naval Air Station when I was ready. If I passed, I could apply to have my commission changed from civil engineering to aviation. He had already arranged with his father to make this transfer. To qualify for the commission and further training, my flying skills and knowledge must be equal to having completed advanced training in the Navy, except for military specialties. The Navy would teach me these in about sixty hours, including carrier landings. Then I would get my wings and go to an operating squadron for 200 more hours, which would make me a 500-hour pilot and ready for any duty the Navy wanted to assign me on a carrier.

The next ten weeks went quickly. I flew all day three days a week; studied for the ground school test the other four days; and spent as many of the remaining hours as possible on the beaches, surfing, swimming, and lying in the sun. I had met several datable girls, and my social circle, which were mostly naval officers I had met through Steve and Jim, increased considerably. We had weekend parties, went dinner dancing at the Royal and Lau Ye Chai's, and enjoyed moonlight swims at little private coves with sandy beaches that were prevalent off Kalanianaole Highway east of

Diamond Head and Kahala Beach. We had picnics at alluring spots like the Blow Hole, which was a rocky beach where ocean waves surged through holes in the volcanic rocks causing geysers of water like whales spouting.

Luaus were the most fun of all. Luaus are Hawaiian parties given in the native manner. First, kanakas (native men), who wore surfing shorts or short sarongs around their waists, dug a long ditch and filled it with lava rock and started a fire. When the rocks were hot and the fire had died down, they layered ti or banana leaves on the rocks and lowered a whole puaa (pig) with the hair scrubbed off onto the leaves, belly-side up. Next the kanakas lined the inside of the pig with leaves and filled it with hot rocks. The entire pig was then buried under more layered leaves and hot rocks. A few hours later, as the wonderful smells began to fan out from under the scorched leaves and the roasting puaa, the drinking, the music, and the dancing, performed by professional men and women hula dancers, began. Nearby, roasts of beef barbecued on spits, and heikaukau (rock crab) and welakaukau (Hawaiian hot stew cooked in calabashes) hung over the fires. In addition to the roasting meats, there was an abundance of other delicious foods: kukui nuts, a-i-apaakai (salt fish), i-a-uahi (smoked fish), and i-a-hau (raw fish), poi, papaya, pineapple, malala, peels of raw sugar cane, all washed down with okulehau (sugar cane wine) and Mai Tais.

While the food cooked, everyone drank, danced and ate the exotic delicacies as they watched the rippling muscles of the half-naked, bronze bodies doing the hula in the flickering fire light under the koa trees. Then the drums began to beat harder and faster as the pig was unearthed, and the guests sat down cross-legged in a big circle for dinner. During dinner the band played and individual performers sang Hawaiian songs and danced hulas in the center of the circle. Sometimes, if they were drunk enough, guests would take off their shoes and jump into the circle and dance, encouraged by the laughing crowd. They were great parties.

****

After about fifty hours of flying the Fleet, my primary training was completed and Myrna give me a test. I had been required to fly the entire time using the altimeter, airspeed indicator, magnetic compass, and oil pressure indicator as the only dashboard instruments. The other instruments were covered with tape. Myrna explained that she did this because she wanted her students to fly "by the seat of their pants, the wind of their face, and the sound of the engine." According to her, it was the only way that one could get the feel of the airplane. For example, wind blowing on your left cheek indicated that you were slipping to the left.

The test included six and eight turn tail spins terminating on a specified heading, hammerhead turns, all sorts of rolls, split "S's," chandelles, loops, inverted flight, Immelmanns and dead stick landings made by slipping over fences into small fields. The cross-country test was to fly solo to the flight strips on Molokai and Maui Islands, land, get the log signed, and return home. The ground school test included trouble-shooting a disabled engine and an hour of questions concerning various procedures. At this point Myrna awarded me my private pilot's license.

I'll always remember the Fleet as the easiest, most stable, responsive, and aerobatic plane I've ever flown. Since it was a biplane covered with doped fabric stretched over an alloy metal frame, it was very light. It was strongly trussed together and had a high-lift air foil with a high power-to-weight ratio. It lifted off the ground at about forty knots, cruised at 100 to 110 knots, stalled at about 35 knots, and landed at about 40 knots. It climbed well over 1500 feet per minute and had no serious faults.

Now it was time to move up to the heavier airplane, the WACO. This plane was a cross-country model, bigger and heavier than the Fleet, with a forward cockpit large enough for two passengers. It was faster than the Fleet, but it was not intended to be especially aerobatic; therefore, it was not as maneuverable as the Fleet but certainly safe enough. It was not a sport plane. The important thing, as far as I was concerned, was its state-of-the-art instrumentation, which included a gyro compass, rate of climb indicator, and artificial horizon. This plane could be flown at night and through clouds, fog, and even rain storms. However, no planes in these days could land or take off without good visibility at the field. In fact, you had to see the ground to find the field. There was a low frequency radio system available for cross-country navigation which was used by airlines, but was used very little by private planes and not at all in Hawaii, which had only a few homing radio beacons at the airports and on mountain peaks. The weekly Pan American seaplane flight from the mainland, *The China Clipper*, used celestial navigation to find its way across the Pacific, supplemented with an unreliable radio homing device called a radio direction finder.

My next fifty flying hours were spent learning instrument flying, working on weather maps, and practicing telegraphy, the standard communication system of the time. Myrna told me the Army and Navy had radios with audio communications in their airplanes for very short range use, either between themselves or to a tower at the air field; however, these radios were expensive, heavy, unreliable, picked up static, and were subject to blanking out when near electrical storms. All airports with traffic control used flashing green and red lights as signals to airplanes taking off or landing. During instrument flight training the student always flew in the front cockpit of the WACO, which was well suited for this work because the seat was lower than usual and the windshield tapered back on the sides, all of which could be conveniently covered with black paper stuck to the inside glass surfaces. Thus, with the top wing overhead, the trainee was in a box, isolated from the wind, the horizon and everything outside.

Without seeing the horizon, feelings, sound, and, to some extent, wind pressure ceased to convey information to the pilot about the airplane's attitude. It has been proven time and time again that a pilot flying blind can fly straight and level for only a minute or two unless he refers to the appropriate instruments and disregards his bodily feelings. The instruments substitute for all the senses. Many a pilot has been killed flying on a dark night or in a fog by following his feelings when the instruments contradicted them. What generally happens in such cases is that the plane stalls and goes into a spin or corkscrew dive and the pilot doesn't know what's happening and can't correct it.

The first few hours of instrument training was a shouting session. I couldn't do anything right, but soon I began to get the knack. The first test I had to pass was to get the plane flying straight and level from any attitude Myrna put it in, including spins. This had to be accomplished by using the needle-ball, airspeed indicator, altimeter and magnetic compass only. When I passed this test to Myrna's satisfaction, she taught me to add the gyro instruments: the compass, artificial horizon, and rate of climb indicator. These made the job much easier, but it was necessary to know both systems in case one failed. Today training to fly an airplane on instruments isn't much different, except that spins aren't included because the planes aren't built to handle the stress. Today we have added radio procedures for navigation, which adds at least 200% in time and 500% in complexity to the training. As I neared thirty-five hours on instruments, Myrna let me fly solo cross-country through clouds, at night, and over the ocean, frequently to other islands. Finally she said it was all right to fly the Stagger Wing Beech biplane with the 450 horse power engine—the ultimate. This plane was similar in most respects to the SNJ, the Navy designation for a Scout trainer which the Navy would use for my checkout test. The SNJ and the Beech flew about the same speed. According to Myrna the SNJ was a little heavier, a little more powerful, and easier to fly. During the next month I put in 100 hours or more on the Beech, going everywhere and doing everything I could in the way of cross-country work and weather flying.

By the first of June I had more than the required 200 hours for the commercial license. Myrna agreed that I was ready and directed me to make an appointment with the local aviation section of the Federal Department of Transportation to take the written examination. The test turned out to be easy—even the telegraphy part. With the written test out of the way, Myrna gave me the flying examination. This test, too, proved to be easy because by then I could handle the Beech like a glove. The test involved mainly safety and emergency procedures, including procedures for communicating with airports by means of light signals and airplane maneuvers. Since Myrna knew I could handle the airplane, the check only took an hour. When we landed, she wrote out the commercial license.

That night Myrna and I went out to dinner at a Kaneohe Restaurant to celebrate. When I dropped her off at home, she reminded me to come back for a refresher before I took the Navy flying exam.

****

During my flight training, I continued to keep in touch with Jim

McCandless. He always seemed glad to hear from me. One day when we were talking, he suggested we call on his sister-in-law, his brother Lincoln's widow. Graciously, she invited us to lunch. She was a charming lady of maybe eighty years, who lived alone on a big estate like Jim's. It was located on Nuuanu Avenue above Oahu Country Club, and it overlooked most of Honolulu. It was a breathless sight. On the day we were there, we could see across Kaiwi Channel to Molokai with its crown of clouds.

Mrs. McCandless showed me room after room filled with Hawaiian art, much of it dating from the nineteenth and very early twentieth centuries. It included clothing, masks, headdresses, spears, surf boards, cooking utensils, musical instruments, and unbelievably beautiful native Hawaiian tapa cloth, which in 1941 was unobtainable. Some tapa cloth was manufactured in small pieces in Tahiti and Samoa, but it scarcely compared to Hawaiian tapa. Like Jim's house, Mrs. McCandless' home was three stories. The top floor was a dance floor and party room. I imagined the gala affairs back in the twenties and earlier, when their careers were at their peak and the white man dominated the closed Hawaiian society in which they all knew one another, belonged to the same club, and divided up all the land among themselves. There is a native Hawaiian saying: "The white man preachers came and made us Christians; and while we were busy looking up at heaven and praying to God, the white man stole all our land."

The luncheon was served on a shaded lanai which captured a panoramic view of most of Honolulu and the ocean. As I remember, we had appetizers of smoked fish, followed by an elaborate salad of local fruits, and Mai Tais.

Later, we walked the grounds to examine a large number of exotic tropical trees and shrubs collected from around the world. There was a hot house sheltering hundreds of species of orchids, which Mrs. McCandless collected as a hobby. I visited the lovely estate twice more before I left Honolulu. A year or two after the war began, Mrs. McCandless died and I have always wondered what happened to her lovely home. I hope it's a public park, but it was probably subdivided.

Aerial view approaching the airport in Hilo, Hawaii, circa 1940.

SEVEN

One Last Vacation

C OMMERCIAL LICENSE IN HAND AND EXPECTING A COMMISSION in the
Navy sometime in August, I had all of July for vacation, which I
figured I'd better take while I had the chance. I still had about a thousand
dollars, which was plenty of money, so I decided to go to Hawaii, the
Big Island, to see the volcanoes and look up my classmate, Howard
Naquin, whose permanent residence was on the Kukuihaele Sugar
Plantation. I knew he was going to medical school on the mainland, but
thought he might be home by the end of June. His father had been the
plantation manager for several years and had answered my inquiry as to
Howard's whereabouts with an invitation to come and visit them any
time, even if Howard wasn't there.

I found an inter-island shuttle boat that was cheap and I booked passage.
The trip took about thirty hours because the boat stopped at Lahaina, Maui,
to load and unload passengers and freight. There were no sleeping quarters
or eating arrangements, except a snack bar, but that was enough for me.
The trip was very rough because that flat-bottom boat slapped and plowed
all the way. The passengers all got sick, and I got no rest. The movement
was more uncomfortable than anything I had ever experienced in an
airplane, but I still didn't get sick. We docked at Lahaina for six hours in
the middle of the night, and I watched the barracuda swimming around the

boat under the flood lights. The next evening we arrived at Hilo, Hawaii, and I was dead tired.

The island of Hawaii is the largest in the Hawaiian chain: about 100 miles long and seventy-five miles wide and about 4,000 square miles in area. It is dominated by three mountains: Mauna Kea, elevation 13,796 feet; Mauna Loa, 13, 680 feet; and Hualali, 8,266 feet. Since these mountains are volcanoes and Mauna Loa is very active, lava covers about 20% of the island. Hawaii gets less rainfall than the other islands, so it is often referred to as the desert island. However, parts of Hawaii, especially the eastern coast, are very lush and heavily vegetated. Hilo is the capitol and the largest city. At the time of my visit, Hilo had a population of 2,500 and the rest of the island was sparsely populated. The principal tourist attractions were the volcanoes. The economy was dominated by sugar plantations and cattle ranches. I had a reservation in the only hotel in Hilo, which wasn't very much, but it was satisfactory. Hilo was strictly a native town, unconcerned with tourism and, therefore, interesting and pleasant. When tourists arrived they were usually met by a bus and whisked away to the Volcano House Hotel at Kilauea. Most of the streets were unpaved and the majority of buildings were single story wooden structures which needed paint. The beautiful tropical trees, shrubs, and flowers that I had seen in Honolulu were everywhere. The markets and stores were generally open to the streets, with babies and small children crying, dogs and pigs sitting around under the tables, and bins of fruit and vegetables, half of which were over-ripe and rotting and gave off a sweet decaying odor.

After a good sleep, I decided to walk around town. As I was sauntering down one of the back streets, I came to an Episcopal church where the pastor was cutting some flowers in a small garden in front. As I came by he straightened up, smiled, and said, "Hello." I stopped and we began a conversation. He was a young missionary-type, maybe thirty years old. He was completing a five-year tour of duty in Hilo and transferring soon to Samoa. In fact, his relief had already arrived and was staying with him in the church living quarters. It ended up that I was invited to dinner. He asked me to call him Joe and that night introduced me to his friend, George. Meeting two Episcopal ministers on a social level was, for me, an unusual experience. As a kid I was always very much subordinated to them because as a child I rang the bells, carried the cross, swept the chapel, counted the money collected from the church goers, and ran errands all day Sunday for the clergy of St. Andrews Church, as well as attended the services. I hated it. I considered the ministers unworldly money grubbers who wanted everything free and somewhat picky—just generally obnoxious. Joe and George were different. Joe had two servants, a cook and housekeeper. We were served martinis and a good home-cooked dinner with plenty of the church's wine. In fact, before dinner was over, I was calling them Saint Joe and Saint George, and they were addressing each other that way also. Both knew I was a renegade Christian and an ex-Episcopalian, but neither ever alluded to it as long as I knew them.

Before the evening was over, the three of us decided to tour the island together, using Saint Joe's car. Two days later, we loaded the car and took off to see Hawaii. Our plan was to drive south from Hilo to Cape Kamukahi and Kalapana to visit the black sand beaches, then backtrack to Keaau and over to Kilauea and the Volcano House where we would stay overnight. From there we would go south again, through the Kau Desert and then turn in a northerly direction across the lava flows to the City of Refuge, a national historical park. We then would continue north to Kealakekua, where Captain Cook was killed in a fight with the Hawaiian natives. After two days there, we planned to visit the McCandless cattle ranch and Kona and then drive across the Parker Ranch, one of the largest cattle ranches in the world, to the Kukuihaele Plantation where the Pacific Sugar Mill was located, and visit the Naquins, with whom we figured we could decorously stay. Eventually we would take the coast highway back to Hilo.

Our first stop, the black sand beach, proved to be marvelous. The narrow strips of black sand were backed by a forest of coconut palms leaning seaward, almost to the surf line. It was here we saw our first hukilau—a long fish net maneuvered in the waist-deep surf by a large number of Hawaiian men forming a tremendous dragnet in a community effort to catch fish. The net was dragged ashore, and the fish that were too small to eat were thrown back in the water. Here and there along the shore, individuals threw small dragnets and speared fish.

We found a place to spend the night in Kaimu and Saint Joe arranged for a native woman to cook us a fresh fish dinner with sweet potatoes. That evening we sat on the beach and drank our martinis and watched the sun go down behind Mauna Loa—the beginning of a ritual we followed for the rest of the trip. The next day we went back the way we came as far as Keaau, where we turned left onto the main highway west to Mokuaweoweo, located at the summit of Mauna Loa, and Kilauea, situated on the lower slope of Mauna Loa at an altitude of 4,000 feet. Both are active volcanoes which erupt every few years. Kilauea is the more active, and even when dormant, growls and smokes with chimneys full of boiling lava, which is frequently visible to visitors. It was in this stage when we arrived. We checked into Volcano House, then went to the museum to hear a lecture given by a ranger. After performing our sunset-watching ritual, we went to dinner and then to an observation platform to see the glowing craters at night.

The next day we headed for the City of Refuge, an ancient religious sanctuary for natives. To get there, we spent several hours passing through great black and reddish lava flows which extended from the top of Mauna Loa, twenty five miles or more, to the sea. Kealakekua, where there is a monument to Captain Cook who died there in 1779, and the City of Refuge were mildly interesting; but since they had no swimming beaches, we kept on going northwest to Kona.

Kona was a sugar port which had one fine hotel on the waterfront, the Kona Inn. Unfortunately, there weren't many sandy beaches in Kona either, but one could swim in the ocean since the shoreline wasn't as rocky as most of the west coast. The Inn was protected by a concrete sea wall, and nearby there was a long wooden wharf used by inter-island steamships for loading and unloading freight. The dining room bar and most of the guest rooms had panoramic views of the sea. Since it was the second week of June, the summer crowds hadn't arrived in the Hawaiian Islands. However, the bartender said it never did get very crowded in Kona, and guests didn't stay long because there wasn't much to do unless one were a deep-sea fisherman. At that time the biggest marlin in the world had been caught off the coast of Kona.

I met Dwight Long in the bar room of the Kona Inn. He'd come to the Inn for lunch. Since we three were the only other people there, we invited him to join us. It turned out that he owned a small sail boat, maybe twenty-five feet long named the Idle Hour, which was anchored in front of the Inn. He was on a single-handed sailing trip around the world. He had started from somewhere in New England, sailed down the Atlantic coast, gone through the Panama Canal, and gotten as far as the Hawaiian Islands. When he got to Oahu, he found that he had been drafted into the Army; so he was vacationing for a last few weeks, like I was, before going into the service. He planned to store his boat in Oahu for the duration.

Dwight made a living as a writer and by giving lectures concerning his personal adventures circumnavigating the world alone in his boat. He was a prolific photographer and was experimenting with underwater photography, which at that time hadn't been commercially developed. He had made his own underwater camera and was in the process of developing a satisfactory underwater illumination system to use with it.

After three days in Kona, we decided to continue on our journey. Before we left, Long invited me to return to Oahu, with him, in his sail boat. He wanted to leave Kona the last of June, which coincided with my plans. Since Long was skin diving and taking pictures under water, I thought maybe he could use some help and I could learn something. I decided to go ahead to see the Naquins, say farewell to my traveling companions, and return to Kona and stay until it was time to go.

The McCandless Ranch was about twenty-five miles north of Puuanahulu. When we arrived at that tiny community we saw a sign pointing down a dirt road; it said, "McCandless Ranch." We headed in that direction. After a few miles of winding road, we came to a ranch house. As we pulled up to the house, a Hawaiian caretaker came over to the car and introduced himself. He said that there were no McCandlesses around at the time but that it was an active ranch which belonged to the Lincoln McCandless estate. He explained that they ran about a thousand head of cattle and said that he'd be glad to show us around, but there wasn't much to see. He suggested we come back in about three months when they'd be receiving new stock, and we could see the animals being delivered, which was done by lowering them in nets over the side of a ship lying off the shore and having them swim to the beach. That would have been interesting to see. We thanked him and went on our way.

We had phoned the Naquins from Kona and advised them that we were arriving that day. We arrived at the plantation late in the afternoon and received a lovely welcome. Mr. Naquin was still working, but Mrs. Naquin met us with great cordiality. She led us to the verandah where we were served a mint julep. We could tell by her accent why we were served the mint juleps rather than the customary mai-tais. She was from Louisiana—a true southern belle. It seemed that she and Mr. Naquin were reared on Louisiana sugar plantations and both had attended Louisiana State University, where he had majored in sugar technology.

The plantation covered thousands of acres and was a self-contained operation. They planted, raised, harvested, and reduced the cane to raw sugar in their own mill; then they loaded and shipped it to California for refinement. Most of the employees, except for the technical or specialized help, were Hawaiian or part Hawaiian and lived in various settlements on the grounds. They had company-provided stores, a school, hospital, churches, and meeting halls. The cane was brought to the mill on a narrow-gauge railway, which also served to transport workers to the fields. I was told that many employees were born, lived, and died on the plantation and that many never left the grounds their entire lives.

The plantation house was designed in the tradition of the antebellum south: a grand mansion with Georgian columns, wide verandahs, screened porches, ceiling fans, a huge dining room, and circular staircases. While we were downing our first drink, Mr. Naquin joined us. He was a fine looking man in his early fifties and was as friendly and cordial as his wife. He sat down and ordered a drink from the houseman and told us that he hoped we could stay a few days, since he had arranged to show us the plantation mill and Waipio Valley. He added that he was sorry that Howard wouldn't be there.

The next few days we leisurely toured the plantation, by both automobile and horseback. We visited the sugar mill, attended a quiet luau given in our honor, and learned a great deal about sugar manufacturing. I was particularly interested in the irrigation system because it used both rainfall and pumped underground water as a source.

The Waipio Valley was on private land and was kept as a refuge or sanctuary for pure-blooded Hawaiians who wanted to live in their own native way, as they had before white men inundated their culture. I'm sure the territorial government was involved, but I don't remember how. The valley was not open to the public, just to anthropologists, scholars, and friends of the Naquins. The only outside help these people received was medical attention and food, if they needed it.

The trip to Waipio Valley was fairly interesting. The natives were somewhat dirty. They lived in thatched huts, cooked on the ground, and had dogs and pigs running in and out of their habitats. Most of the clothing they wore, however, was not particularly native. We were told that the people were self-sufficient and grew most of their own food, principally sweet potatoes and taro root which is pounded into poi. They also made fishing nets and hukilaus from local fibers and vines. Although we saw some very nice lei and hat bands woven with feathers, we were asked not to trade with the natives; so we didn't buy any artifacts.

After being guests for four days, we decided it was time to go: Joe and George back to Hilo and I back to Kona. One of the plantation foremen was driving to Kona, and I arranged to ride with him. On the eve of our departure, the Naquins assembled a small Hawaiian band to play for us during cocktail hour. This group didn't play current popular songs since they were considered "tinpan alley." Instead, they played some of the ancient chants which were very different, very enjoyable, and not often heard. The next morning after profusely thanking the Naquins for their hospitality, Joe, George, and I bade our farewells to each other and went our separate ways. I arrived in Kona about lunch time. The Inn's guest list was bigger, but still small, and Dwight Long's boat was still anchored in front. After talking to Dwight and setting the departure date, I told the manager I'd be there about ten days. The manager asked me if I'd consider tending bar during that time since he'd lost a bartender and it would take a few days to find a new one. He offered to trade me a room for the job. I agreed as long as I worked the 4:00 p.m.-to-midnight shift. I wanted to help Dwight get the boat ready in the morning and early afternoon and to do some swimming and surfing. Although the surfing conditions weren't particularly good, I knew that it might be my last chance—and it just about was!

Being a bartender was a new job for me. I knew how to mix the common drinks, but there were some unusual tropical drinks that originated in Hawaii about which I knew nothing. The owner solved the problem by giving me a book on the subject, written by Victor Bourgeon, owner of Trader Vic's. Soon I was making zombies, blue lagoons, and Mai Tais like a pro. As a bartender, I found myself in a new position—one of always being expected to answer all sorts of questions and talk to anyone who would start a conversation. I usually said I was born in Shanghai and was a soldier of fortune working my way around the world. Normally this brought a laugh, but not always.

One evening I was fascinating an unsuspecting elderly couple with one of my really wild stories when I heard laughter coming from down the bar. I hadn't seen the couple come in so I moved toward them to take their order. The source of the laughter was a lady who looked at me and said, "You liar!" It was Jean Dodge, an ex-girlfriend from Stanford. She was with her new husband George Dole (the pineapple Dole). She couldn't stop laughing and neither could I. I have since heard that after divorcing several husbands, she made her permanent home in Paris.

When I wasn't bartending, I was helping Dwight clean up and provision his boat. I knew nothing about sailing, so it was an opportunity to learn. We scrubbed the bottom, repaired the rigging, painted the interior, greased, and rubbed. He taught me how to tie knots and introduced me to diving goggles. (Masks and snorkels hadn't been invented yet.) All this time the boat was riding at anchor. I generally swam out to it and back to shore for exercise. It was with the goggles that I got my first look at coral and the wonderful Hawaiian fish. I had been swimming in the ocean and surfing since I was twelve years old, but I had no idea what lay beneath me. It really opened for me a new domain of which I still never tire. When I got back to Honolulu, I bought a couple pairs of goggles and carried them with me all through the war.

The first leg of our boat trip was to Lahaina, Maui, which was about 100 miles from Kona. The trade winds were blowing hard from the northeast and we calculated they would catch us broadside for most of the trip. In sailing, this is called a beam reach, which is the fastest point of sail and also very wet. Dwight figured it would take thirty hours since the Idle Hour was such a small boat–meaning slow. We left Kona at the break of dawn with very little wind and headed southwest into the Alenuihaha Channel, which separates Hawaii from Maui. Gradually the wind picked up and the port rail went down into the water. As we turned on to our course, we shortened sail and settled down to a steady bearing that made the trip almost a straight shot. It was my first sail and I loved it (although not as well as flying). Dwight had me steer for the first hour as he cleaned up the boat; then we took turns on the tiller. The night was black and the water rough, so we wore life jackets, and the helmsman tied himself to the boat so he couldn't fall out while the other person slept. I couldn't sleep at all in that rolling, pitching boat., but of course, Dwight had no problem. I couldn't, and still can't, imagine anyone going around the world alone and doing this day after day. We sailed into Lahaina Marina just before noon as scheduled. Dwight went ashore and I went to bed. That night we had dinner at the Banyan Tree Cafe and walked around town. Like Hilo, Lahaina was a very small little waterfront shack town with a population of maybe 1,000. The few tourists that stopped there had come to see Haleakala, the volcano crater. Lahaina served mostly as a secondary port for the agricultural business on the western side of the island. The main port, Kahului, was on the eastern side of the island.

The trip to Honolulu from Maui was more of the same and took about twenty-four hours. We arrived in the yacht basin about noon. I helped Dwight put the boat into shape and took my leave. It was the Fourth of July, 1941.

The author spent many hours honing his flying skills in Navy SNJ trainers like these.

EIGHT

The Navy

WHEN I GOT TO THE MAKIKI HOTEL, I FOUND MY DRAFT notice in the mail and also a letter from the Navy saying my application was in order and being processed. The next day I went to the draft board with my notice and the letter from the Navy to explain the situation. To my amazement, they refused to listen and told me I was to be inducted into the Army. I was told to take the physical right then and there and to report to Schofield Barracks. To their consternation I refused to take the physical and headed for Jim Robison at the Navy Recruiting Office. Jim wasn't there. The chief said that he'd take care of the situation but that I should contact Robison, who was anxious to see me. When I phoned Jim the next day, he told me everything was set. Each aviation candidate with a commercial license who had been accepted by the Navy would be trained on an individual basis at Ewa Marine Air Station or Ford Island Naval Air Station. Jim thought, however, it would be wise to wait until the first of August to qualify so that my aviation qualification was completed just before I got the CEC (Civil Engineer Corps) commission; then I could be transferred as an officer. I didn't understand the details, but I left that to Jim. As I look back on it now, Robison had some strong pull with his father, and it was very nice of him to use it to help me out. I was lucky to have met him.

I spent the rest of July working on my sun tan, surfing at Waikiki, and girl-chasing on what must have been the best hunting grounds in the world. The easiest approach was to find a newly arrived young lady, who had rented a surf board without an instructor and was, of course, floundering. "Hi!, let me show you how." That was all there was to it. In those days "ladies" didn't go to cocktail lounges alone, and I was only interested in "ladies." I never knew a girl for more than a few days because she was always a tourist. This situation was fine because I wasn't interested in anything serious. During the last week of July, I made my application for naval aviation through Jim Robison. In three or four days I received a reply. At the beginning of August, I was to report to the Ewa Marine Air Station to take a written and oral exam, followed immediately by an examination aloft, and then a cross-country air trip.

First I took the oral exam, which is a pre-qualification for the written. The officer that interviewed me was a Marine captain who questioned me about my education, family background, reasons for joining the service, and, of course, my flying experience. He looked a little skeptical, but said, "Okay, let's go fly."

The captain asked me whether I had brought any flying gear, which I had. Then he handed me a parachute, and we walked out to an N3N biplane. The captain motioned me into the front seat and told me where to taxi for take-off. My instructions were to climb over the ocean to 4,000 feet and show him what I could do.

The N3N was very similar to the Fleet: simply a military version of the same plane beefed up for rougher use. I went through a complete aerobatics routine terminating with a hammer-head followed by an Immelmann, after which he shook the controls indicating he was taking over to fly us back to the airfield. We entered the downwind leg of the landing pattern in military style and he shook the controls again, which meant that I was to land it. On the voice tube he shouted, "On the numbers," which meant he wanted a spot-landing on the numbers marking the end of the runway. The landing was easy enough. When we got out of the plane, all he said was to come back tomorrow at the same time to take a written exam, the same one then used at Pensacola at the conclusion of basic training.

The next day after I finished the exam, the Captain spent a couple of hours introducing me to military procedures. He described military landing patterns, demonstrated use of the voice radio, discussed in detail the Navy systems for designating airplanes and squadrons, and explained a few military routines that he felt I should know including how to go about obtaining military weather briefings and how to file military flight plans. We then checked out an SNJ-2 (Scout Trainer, North American—Model 2), the standard Navy advanced trainer, for some "touch-and-go's" (take off and landing practice). The SNJ-2 was my first experience flying a monoplane and a plane with retractable landing gear. For initial familiarization the Captain went through the cockpit instruments and controls with me. He told me the engine settings and speeds to use with an SNJ, which I wrote on a card, and he reminded me that we were in a retractable landing gear airplane. I radioed the tower, taxied into position, and took off. The plane climbed well; but after the Beech biplane, it seemed heavier and less responsive. We climbed out over the ocean where I practiced maneuvering until I got the feel. Then, on the captain's orders, I headed back to the field. I called the tower, got into the pattern, went through the check list, and made a rather bumpy landing after which we pulled off the runway onto a taxi-way. The captain then gave me some instructions about how the plane should be handled, tips on landing, and a reminder that the tail wheel couldn't be used for steering because it was designed for landing on aircraft carriers. The wheel was either in a castor mode or fixed straight ahead, a little different than I was used to. For the next couple of hours we practiced landings and take-offs until I felt reasonably comfortable.

When we were through, the captain gave me a set of navigation instruments, some maps, and some forms for filing flight plans He told me to be back at 0800 the following morning with a complete cross-country navigational plot—including weather reports—for a trip to Maui, Hawaii, Molokai, and return. He would give no help before the flight or in route. I was on my own. If I got off course or couldn't find the airport, I would be washed out. We would use the SNJ-2.

The SNJ Scout Trainer was powered by a 550 hp WASP radial engine. It cruised at about 180 knots and had a range of 900 miles. It was about the size and configuration of the current scout dive bombers, the SB2U2 (Scout Bomber Vought Sikorsky Vindicator) and the new SBD (Scout Bomber Douglas Dauntless), only not as heavy and with about half the power. They all carried two people in tandem position and the cockpits were covered with a sliding greenhouse canopy. The SNJ was used for advanced training by squadron five at Pensacola and, like all military aircraft, was aerobatic. The next step up the ladder from this was the operational fighting plane. The next morning the captain looked over my navigational plans, wind calculations, and estimated times of arrival. He made a few comments and said, "Okay, let's go." I asked him if I should fly through the clouds. "Don't ask me; use your judgement. That's why we're doing this," he responded.

The trip to Maui was uneventful. The first island we would come to, Molokai, was soon in sight, so we couldn't be very far off course. I flew at about 5,000 feet, passing just north of Molokai and straight through occasional clouds, to Kahului Airport on Maui. I radioed the tower and made an almost straight-in approach followed by a good landing. The second leg of the flight to Hilo, Hawaii, was very much the same as the first leg, except that we ran into rain and heavy mist as we flew over the shorelines north of Maui and Hawaii. It was not frontal rain but just a tropical precipitation from a high cloud deck, which was typical of Hawaiian weather and usually not mentioned in the forecast. Here is where I got a chance to show the captain I could fly instruments. We landed at General Lyman Field, Hilo, in the mist and rain. The trip had taken about two hours.

We had coffee at Hilo. By the time we were ready to leave, the weather had cleared and the air was soft and free of dust. Everything looked clean and crystal clear.

"Okay, McCandless, plot a different course home and do it in fifteen minutes." The captain's orders were no surprise since I was supposed to be ready for anything connected with flying.

I drew a line straight across the island of Hawaii: from Hilo, over Humuula saddle, between Mauna Loa and Mauna Kea, to Kawaihae Bay on the west coast, then a straight line across the ocean to home port in Honolulu. I figured we would miss the rain, which was floating north on a southernly wind. I calculated that the safe altitude to fly would be about 7,500 feet and we would keep out of the clouds and clear the highest land mass on our route by about 1,500 feet. After we got over the ocean, we would always stay within gliding distance of land. There wasn't any point in trying to get a weather report - we knew more than the weather forecaster did. I explained to the captain why I chose this route and he approved.

"Well, Mac, we'll see if you're right." We took off and everything was fine until we got opposite Lanai, where we ran into rain again and were forced back to flying on instruments. When we arrived in the rain at Ewa, the visibility was sufficient to land. As we entered the officer's club for a drink, the Captain said, "Everything is fine. I'll send the papers in tomorrow."

On August 12, the Navy recruiting office called to tell me my commission as an ensign in the Civil Engineer Corps of the U.S. Navy had arrived and that I was to come down and be sworn in. Immediately after I was sworn in, I bought a couple of khaki Navy uniforms, put one on, and went to a photographer to have pictures taken to send to my family. The next day I reported for duty at Navy Headquarters, Pearl Harbor, and was assigned temporary duty with the Public Works Department at Ford Island.

Marine Corps Air Station Ewa, Oahu, Hawaii, shortly after commissioning, Feb. 1941, showing the crow's nest of the mooring mast converted into the airstrip's control tower.

NINE

Military Flight Indoctrination

O N AUGUST 21 I GOT ANOTHER CALL FROM THE RECRUITING office. I had received orders that transferred me from engineering to an aviation designation and reassigned me from my position in the Public Works Department to the commanding officer on Ford Island Naval Air Station for military flying indoctrination. The commanding officer directed me to the Marine Air Corps Air Station, Ewa, where I was assigned living quarters with a Marine, second lieutenant. I would be the only naval officer in the program.

Ewa was an operational Marine Corps air station; however, because of the training rush, a number of new Marine pilots from Pensacola were being sent to operating squadrons in Hawaii to finish their training. Some of these pilots had only 275 flying hours instead of the normal 500. None of the pilots were qualified to land on aircraft carriers, and the scout bomber pilots had never made a dive on a target. Accordingly, two training squadrons had been established at Ewa to make these pilots operational, one squadron for fighters and one for dive bombers. I was assigned to the dive bomber squadron, which was fine with me. I could fly as well as my contemporaries, even though they had "wings" and I didn't, and I preferred not to go to fighters. I'd rather "carry the mail" in an attack plane—it seemed more glamorous. The first fifty hours of training concentrated on the transition from training planes to operational ones—the kind flown in combat. The fighter students were transferred to the F2A Brewster Buffalos and the scout bomber types to SB2U2 Vought Sikorskys Vindicators. The curriculum for both of us focused mainly on flying in formation and practicing carrier landings. Formation training included practicing various formations, changing from one formation to another on command, and holding one position hour after hour while watching the next plane's wing tip a few feet away. There was no instructor in the plane; he flew above the squadron, radioing commands. One student pilot acted as a squadron leader around whom the rest of the squadron formed.

Landing an airplane on an aircraft carrier requires a great deal of accuracy and skill on the part of the pilot. The idea is to approach the ship from the stern and land on the main deck in such a manner that a hook hanging from the tail of the plane engages one of several arrester cables laid laterally across the deck. These cables bring the airplane to a stop. A short landing means crashing into the stern of the ship. A long landing means bouncing, bolting, and either smashing into a safety net or skidding overboard into the ocean. Any one of these could be a killer. Carrier landing training, accordingly, was not initially carried out on a ship, but on an airfield. At the end of the runway, a carrier deck was laid out in white paint with imaginary cables painted in yellow. Just as on a ship, the signalman took position off the left hand corner of the runway to advise the approaching airplane of his position. The technique was to stall the plane two or three seconds before making a three point touch-down on the correct spot - in other words, a very accurate and precise landing.

We flew five hours in the morning, five days a week. In the afternoon we spent four hours in a classroom, dive bomber pilots together with the fighter pilots. We listened to lectures and worked problems concerning tactics, survival, navigation, ordinance, gunnery, Navy regulation, radio communications, scouting and observation procedures, and a few other subjects.

At the 0630 daily briefing on September 20,1941, my instructor, Captain Fletcher Brown, informed me that I would be making my first carrier landing that day on CV-2, the Lexington , and that I would be riding alone. I can remember the surge of adrenaline to my head and the trembling of my hands that accompanied the excitement as I took off. About a half hour later, I called the Lexington and got approval to enter the upwind leg of the flight pattern on the starboard side. I opened the canopy, dropped the landing gear flaps and tail hook, then circled around the bow, came downwind on the port side, and circled into the final approach. Again, the adrenaline surged, and I was seeing everything in a finally climaxed focus of crystal clarity that was like slow motion. I later called that feeling the "combat high." I remember coaching myself, "steady as you go...left wing up...a little starboard...nose down," as I watched the signalman standing in his box that hung out on the port stern, his arms outstretched with orange paddles visually telegraphing me my position. Suddenly he folded his arms across his throat and quickly uncrossed them:"Cut!" I pulled back the throttle to idle, pulled up the nose into a stall, and felt a sudden, jolting, vertical crash; then I felt the pressure of a full "G" on my body as I pushed against the seat harness during the sudden stop. Up with the flaps as the deck crew swarmed around unhooking the plane. I looked around, and Brown, who had flown in ahead of me, was standing on my wing with his hand extended.

"Congratulations!" he said. "Your wings—tomorrow! Now, I want to see three more landings; then we'll go home." Taking off was a cinch, but the three landings were each as exciting as the first.

That evening I bought everybody in the Marine officer's club booze until closing time. From the size of the bill, I discovered that Marine aviators are real drinkers. The next day, September 21,1941, Lt. Col. Claude A. Larkin, U.S.M.C., called me into his office and, in the presence of Capt. Brown, pinned on the golden wings.

Fletcher Brown was a truly professional Marine and a fine military aviator. He eventually became an intimate friend. He was twenty-six years old, unmarried, a graduate of Miami University, Pensacola trained, and believed that naval aviators (Marines were naval aviators) were the best airmen in the world. He'd fight anybody who suggested they weren't. Sometimes during cocktail hour, about 5:00 p.m. when the classroom work was finished, he and I would start talking shop. Subjects ranged from military philosophy (Clauswitz, JFC Fuller, Billy Mitchell) to air tactics and airplane maintenance. The conversations frequently lasted through dinner. Later when the cacophonic noise rising from the adjacent bar room precluded further talk, we usually joined the others at the bar. Other times after dinner, we would saunter around the airfield in the tropical twilight, deep in conversation, or we'd go down to the shop where the Marine aviation mechanics were busy getting the planes cleaned and tuned for the next day's run. It was here I began to learn how Marines viewed their service. In contrast to Marine pilots, Navy pilots didn't have a chance to work on their own planes because they were part of a much larger, more formal organization that was highly departmentalized and, therefore, was not conducive to interchanging job roles. In the Navy, a pilot was a pilot and a mechanic was a mechanic. Consequently, the pilot's attitude was that he would fly and fight the planes, but didn't care to work on them. Conversely, many Marine pilots insisted on tuning the engines and adjusting the bore sightings of the guns of their own airplanes and frequently became expert mechanics. Often on the evening walk we would stop and talk to a pilot who was working on his plane, using a flash light for illumination like we as kids used to work on our cars.

Of course, these flying Marines were from the old school, the prewar regulars who in 1940 totaled 245, and all knew each other like fraternity brothers. They unanimously agreed that naval aviation considered them poor cousins. They were handed the obsolete or tired airplanes the Navy didn't want and which the Navy replaced with new planes. Since I was the only naval officer around, I was on the receiving end of some of their animosity.

One evening I was sitting at the small bar nursing a martini when a Marine lieutenant sat down beside me and exclaimed in a loud voice, "Navy officers stink! They won't fight!."

I shouted back, "Here's one that will!" and knocked him and the stool over.

Instead of the bystanders grabbing and holding us, they formed a circle and started yelling for the Marine, "Come on, Joe. Get him! Let's see you fight, swabby."

I leaped on him to keep him from getting up. We rolled over and over in a clinch across the floor, knocking over chairs and the hat stand in the corner.

Finally, a lieutenant colonel shouted, "Attention!" We both quit and stood rigidly at attention. "Shake hands," he said quietly, which we did. Had this been a Navy officer's club, such conduct would have been unthinkable. I'm not sure what would have happened, but probably we'd have been barred from the club for several months. At Ewa, this turned out to be a fairly common occurrence. Marines were basically trained as infantry soldiers before they became flyers, and they were told they were tough. They just liked to fight. If there wasn't an enemy to fight, they'd fight one another!

The Vought SB2U Vindicator was a carrier-based dive bomber developed for the United States Navy in the 1930s, the first monoplane in this role.

TEN

The Naval Aviator

I N OCTOBER OF 1941, MARINE AIR STATION EWA was located on the west side of the Pearl Harbor entrance, and it was the headquarters of MAG (Marine Air Group) 21. Ewa consisted of barracks, mess halls, shops, warehouses, sick bay, the officer's club, and of a couple of dozen corrugated metal buildings which served as bachelor officers' quarters. Two paved airstrips located at right angles to make allowances for local wind shifts filled out the picture. The entire installation consisted of nothing but concrete, asphalt, steel, and bare ground. It had the dreary look of a run-down industrial park, except that it was fairly clean and orderly. Compared to other Hawaiian military air bases, with their white concrete buildings, immaculate lawns, lavish officers' clubs, and thousands of men, Ewa Marine Air Station seemed grossly neglected. In 1941 the entire U.S. Marine Corps had only 204 operational airplanes. Of these, about one-half were stationed in the Atlantic and the other half in the Pacific. Forty of the one-hundred or so planes in the Pacific were located at Ewa Marine Air Station, Hawaii. The rest were divided among Wake Island and the aircraft carriers Lexington and Saratoga.

The Navy, on the other hand, had 5,000 operational aircraft; 1,500 of them, including 250 planes stationed on ships, were stationed in Hawaii.

All of these Navy aircraft and their crews had to be maintained by and housed in the shops and living quarters existing in two naval air stations in Hawaii: NAS Pearl Harbor and NAS Kaneohe. Thus, the emphasis on building large, modern, permanent bases providing excellent shopping, recreational, and living facilities can be understood.

However, the Marines didn't see the situation this way. They were very aware of their second-rate facilities and resented naval aviation. Later in the war, however, the Marines were supplied with the newest and best planes available. One thing for sure, Marine aviators proudly believed they belonged to a very elite, exclusive club; and in a way, they did.

In 1941, naval aviators were initially trained to fly either single-engine or multi-engined airplanes. Additionally, all were trained to fly both seaplanes and land planes and could fly a carrier-type airplane on and off a carrier. Generally, most aviators, as they became seasoned and had the time, learned to fly anything the Navy had by teaching one another in their spare time. Thus, a trained fighter pilot could usually fly a twin-engine seaplane safely, if not proficiently. It was also naval doctrine to have all carrier-type pilots learn each others' tactics and to have actually put in some time flying each type of plane in mock battle, which was a good way of teaching how to evade an enemy as well as to attack him.

Each aircraft carrier was equipped with one air group, comprised of thirty-six fighters, eighteen scouts, eighteen dive bombers, and eighteen torpedo planes. The air group was lead by an air group commander, who in turn was responsible to a fleet or task force air officer who managed several air groups. As far as the air group was concerned, the captain of the ship might be considered as the operator of a hotel and shop. If an air group completed a six months tour of duty or got badly mauled, it would usually be replaced by a fresh new group, but the ship personnel remained the same. In 1941, there was a classic procedure for a United States carrier attacking an enemy carrier. When the U. S. carrier came into range of the enemy carrier, eighteen fighters would go aloft to perform combat air patrol duty (CAP). The planes climbed to 25,000 or 30, 000 feet and orbited their mother carrier on about a ten-mile radius to fend off incoming attacking enemy airplanes. They concentrated, of course, on bombers and torpedo planes which could injure the ship. This was not all that easy since the incoming enemy bombers had their own fighter escorts which had to be gotten out of the way first. The next planes to take off from the U.S. carriers were the eighteen torpedo planes, eighteen dive bombers, and maybe some scouts who would also dive bomb. The last to go aloft were usually the eighteen fighters who would escort our bombers to their destination. The fighters took off last and, on the return, landed first because they carried less fuel and burned more.

The United States air group would approach the enemy, flying in three layers: the escort fighters at 30,000 feet, the dive bombers at 20,000 feet, and the torpedo planes at about 12,000 feet. As the group approached the target, the escort went after the enemy's CAP fighters. The torpedo planes dropped to 500 feet and started a long, straight, two-mile run at the enemy carrier's broadside. They dropped their torpedoes when they were about a half-mile away. Torpedo bombing turned out to be the most dangerous job in naval aviation because the torpedo plane, in its long straight run, was not only a stable target for a ship's anti-aircraft fire, but also an easy target for the attacking enemy fighters.

Meanwhile, the dive bombers dropped to 15,000 feet, lined up on their target, and pushed over into a 70-degree dive at a speed of about 275 miles per hour. From between 1,500 and 2,500 feet above the water, they dropped their 1,000-pound bombs on the enemy ship's deck, leveling out at a minimum of 750 feet and pulling about five G's on the plane and crew, who frequently blacked out momentarily. After straightening out, they ran for friendly fighter cover.

Dive bombing was the most rugged job in flying. It was not as dangerous as torpedo bombing, however, because the anti-aircraft guns on the enemy's ship had a hard time hitting a target coming almost straight down at high speed and the dive only lasted about 30 seconds. From the aviator's point of view, dive bombing was the most productive job in naval aviation. The dive bomber was a very successful weapon system because it was the most accurate of all the bombers in any military service. U.S. Navy dive bombers were credited with sinking over 300,000 tons of shipping and eighteen major Japanese war ships, including six large carriers—more than was credited to the entire United States submarine fleet or any other single weapon system.

The Army system of horizontal bombing, unless flown at treetop height, proved to be almost worthless at pin-pointing a small target like a ship. Naval torpedo bombing, using the tactics current at that time, was eventually discontinued because it was not cost-effective. A high percentage of planes were shot down and very few hits on enemy targets were ever made The operational planes which we were being trained in were the Brewster F2A Buffalo fighter and the Vought Sikorsky SB2U Vindicator dive bomber. These planes had been in service since the mid-thirties and were gradually being replaced by the new and much improved Grumman F4F Wildcat fighter and the Douglas SBD Dauntless dive bomber. In 1941, Naval aviation was still in the middle of the replacement program, and MAG 21 hadn't received the new planes.

The Buffalo was, in a way, the first modern Navy fighter. It was an all-metal monoplane, except for fabric covered control surfaces. With an airspeed of over 325 knots, it was very fast compared with the airplanes it replaced. It was highly maneuverable, light on the controls, and fun to fly. Its deficiencies included no protective armor for the pilot, no self-sealing gas tanks, and poor performance at altitudes over 20,000 feet because the engine was not supercharged. Additionally, the Buffalo required high maintenance and, for a carrier plane, had a weak undercarriage which frequently collapsed when the plane caught the wire. The Buffalo also had a vicious sudden left-hand roll, which whipped into a spin if the pilot wasn't very careful to avoid pulling too many G's as he pulled out of a steep dive. However, this characteristic was not uncommon in other military planes.

The deficiencies of the Buffalo were corrected in the new F4F Wildcat, which was rough, tough, easy to fly, and performed well with its three-speed, two-stage supercharger. The plane had no bad habits except a tendency to ground loop easily because of its narrow undercarriage. The Wildcat was the first of the famous "iron works gang" that Grumman built, which included the great F6F fighter and the TBF bomber. The Wildcat could recover from a ten-turn spin in a half revolution. It has been said that no other military plane in any service could do better than that.

The SB2U Vindicator, also known by the Marines as the "Vibrator," was a part-metal and part-fabric two-seat dive bomber which, like all small combat planes, had a greenhouse sliding canopy that covered the pilot in the front seat and extended back over the gunner. The canopy could be opened and closed at both ends. Normally in those days, all Navy combat planes took off, landed, and fought with the canopies open, so the crew could exit in a hurry if the plane got in trouble. These canopies slid on runners like a sliding door, and any damage to the slides made the canopies ˙ inoperable. The Vindicator was an inherently good flying airplane powered by an 875-horsepower engine. It had a cruising speed of 227 miles per hour and a range of 700 miles when it carried two fifty-gallon drop tanks. It could carry a 1,500-pound bomb load, but a 1,000-pound load was the norm. The Marine Corp version of the Vindicator was the SB2U-3, which had a range of 1200 miles and was considered a "flying fuel tank." Of course, when fully loaded with fuel, it sacrificed bomb load and was used as a scout.

There were three major problems with the Vindicator. The first was that it had no performance carrying a 1,000-pound bomb over 12,000 feet, which was way too low considering that the state-of-the-art fighters were flying at 30,000 feet, giving them a tremendous tactical advantage. The second problem was that in order to maintain a dive without exceeding the plane's strength, it had to drop the landing gear first and then maintain a diving speed of about 225 miles per hour at an angle of no more than 45 degrees. The steeper the dive, the better the chance of hitting the target, and a 70-degree dive was considered the optimum. The Vindicator's third problem was the absence of protective armor for the crew.

The replacement for the SB2U Vindicator was the new and greatly improved SBD Douglas Dauntless scout bomber. This was an all metal two-place monoplane, with a pilot in the front seat and a gunner riding in the backseat. The gunner had a swiveling set of twin machine guns, and the pilot had thirty caliber machine guns located in the cowl. The Dauntless had a 30,000-foot ceiling and an 860-mile range without drop tanks. It carried a 1,000-pound bomb, had a top speed of 250 mph, and cruised at about 225 mph. The Dauntless had heavily armored cockpits, self-sealing fuel tanks, and bullet-proof windshields. It was a pilot's airplane. It dove at 276 mph, using diving flaps at an angle of 70 degrees or steeper. In fact, it could safely go straight down and withstand the pull-out forces since it was stressed for over five Gs. The Dauntless was rugged, very stable, dependable, versatile, and easy to fly. It's been said by naval aviators that it was the most stable heavy ordinance delivery platform used in World War II naval aviation.

The next 200 hours of operational training were demanding, rugged, and fun. There was no worry about washing out since we were all qualified pilots, but we still couldn't relax. We had to become proficient in all the disciplines we'd been taught: carrier landing, instrument flying, aerobatics, dive bombing, and the toughest thing of all, night carrier landings. Aviation combat tactics were invented during World War I and refined during the 1920s and 1930s. However, they had been developed by practicing mock combat with our own airplanes. It turned out that real enemy planes had far different characteristics than ours. For instance, Japanese Zero fighters, assuming the pilots were of equal ability, were much more maneuverable than any fighter the United States had when World War II started. Consequently, new tactics had to be developed to fight successfully. Unfortunately, they had to be worked out the hard way—in real combat.

Major Ira Kimes (United States Marine Corps), skipper of Marine Corps Bombing Squadron 232, was our chief instructor. To complete the required 200 hours of combat training, Major Kimes assigned me to fighter training for my first fifty hours. He stressed two musts for fighter pilots who wanted to stay alive: get altitude advantage and constantly scan the surrounding air space. The altitude advantage provides visibility of what's below and positive overtaking acceleration. Constant scanning protects one from surprise attack. To go into much detail about tactics would require writing a book, so I'll give only a couple of examples.

The idea was constant practice to hone the edge and produce the best fighting pilots possible. The instructor would detail one Buffalo fighter as a target and another as an attacking aircraft. Both aircraft would be assigned a given heading and altitude. The attacking aircraft would fly 1,000 to 2,000 feet ahead and 4,000 feet to one side. On signal from the instructor, the

The SBD Dauntless was a World War II American naval scout plane and dive bomber manufactured by Douglas Aircraft from 1940 through 1944.

attacking aircraft would start what was called "a high side run" on the target. If the target was on the left side, the attacking aircraft would roll into a left nose-down turn, always keeping the target in sight. In the Buffalo the speed would build up to about 350 knots. The ideal run would end up with the attacking aircraft approaching the target at about the same altitude, or slightly below (always below if you were attacking a dive bomber with a rear gunner) moving in at a four o'clock position from the target aircraft. As the attacking pilot starts his run, he eases off on the throttle, then adds back full throttle as he closes on the target. Care must be taken to prevent pulling too many G's when pulling out of the dive, thereby, bleeding off the speed. If all goes well, the attacker passes under the tail of the target and will have sufficient speed to regain his attacking position on the other side and then repeat the process. Once the basic attack maneuver was learned, the target was instructed to defend himself by turning into the attacker. If the aircraft being attacked saw the attacker in time, he two choices: turn away and dive; or wait until the attacker had committed himself, then the defender turns into him just before he gets into firing position, and lets him have it with his guns. (Most guns were bore-sighted to converge fire at 200 to 250 yards ahead of the aircraft.)

Another defense was the split-S, which was frequently used when the defender spotted the enemy approaching head-on at a lower altitude. The defender waited until the enemy was almost under him, then rolled into an inverted position, and dove from above. All this started the dog fight. Of course the objective in any dog fight was to gain an advantageous position for firing at the enemy from behind. After the first pass, the opponent would do everything in his power to prevent another one. This is why a small turning radius was so important in the fighter airplanes. This attempt at strenuous evasion usually ended up with one or the other finally getting on the tail of the opponent. Once this happened, the plane in front was in dire peril. Trying to hold an attack position until the enemy was shot down required all of the flying skill the attacking pilot possessed.

Evasive tactics by the defender included rolls, Immelmanns, chandelles, slips, skids, sudden power changes, and vertical stalls. The only way to keep from being hit was to change positions constantly. If your plane had the speed advantage and the enemy was on your tail, the smart thing to do was to nose over and dive as fast as you could. If you couldn't run, one maneuver was to pull up in a vertical climb and suddenly decrease power. The chasing aircraft would then have to take immediate evasive action to avoid a collision. Of course if he didn't, you were both in trouble. Once I did this very clumsily and fell over in an inverted spin, nearly colliding with my adversary. Needless to say, I got a severe and deserved reprimand from the instructor.

Probably the most thrilling thing I can remember was landing on a carrier at night. This was the real stomach flip-flopper—the sweating hands routine accompanied by excruciating anxiety. These landings were much more exacting than day landings because you couldn't see the deck until you were on base leg turning into final approach. Then all you could see were the two rows of very dim lights outlining the carrier deck and lights on the signal paddles of the landing signal officer. For this period of time, your life was entirely in his hands. Needless to say, the Navy kept night operations to a minimum because of accidents. However, I believed it safer to stay proficient in night landings in case there were ever a chance of having to do one in combat, and of course, there was. Consequently, I did night landings at every opportunity.

The last twenty-five hours of bombing practice were accomplished flying Dauntlesses instead of Vindicators—and what a change! The Dauntless' 75-degree dive was very different from the Vindicator's 45-degree dive and had a much more exciting pull-out. There was always a complete momentary blackout when pulling out of a dive, but it was also much easier to hit the target.

Bombing practice was carried out by bombing targets located on the Hawaiian Island of Kahoolawe off Maui. Normal operational training required fifty practice dives. I had already made a few practice dives, but not with ammunition. In practice we used 500-pound bomb cases filled with colored flour. The instructor, who was flying in circles over the target, observed the location of each shot.

A dive-bombing squadron was composed of three divisions of two three-plane sections. Thus the aircraft flew in groups of three. This formation could put up a reasonable defense against attacking fighters by grouping three swiveling twin machine guns at an attacker. Attack dives were initiated by the leader at about 15,000 feet and from a down-sun and up-wind position if possible. The leader's signal to attack was to kick his rudder back and forth. By this time all canopies had been opened and the rear seat men were facing aft with their machine guns unlimbered and cocked, ready to go. The diving pilot then throttled back and lifted the nose of the plane slightly above the horizon to an almost stalled position. The lever marked "D" at his right hand was operated, opening the dive and landing flaps. The pilot then rolled the plane over on its side, almost inverted, and peeled off, following the plane ahead down in a 70 to 75-degree angle dive toward the target at 276 miles per hour. The crutch gear was then released, swinging the bomb out and down to clear the propeller arc. In the half minute or so of descent, the target was lined up in the cross hairs of the sight and kept there by adjusting the ailerons and rudder. Drift and side slipping were corrected by referring to a bubble tube in the gun sight and keeping the bubble centered. The engine was kept revving over to insure instant pick-up when required. At the selected height—between 1,500 and 2,500 feet—the bomb was released manually by actuating a lever under the lefthand throttle console. On release of the bomb, the throttle was opened up full, the stick pulled back, the dive flaps retracted, and the Dauntless hurtled out, clear of the target, to reform away from the action zone, and hopefully find fighter cover. At pull out pilots were experiencing up to five G's pressure against the backrest.

As I described earlier, air carrier groups consisted of two squadrons of fighters, a squadron of torpedo planes, a squadron of bombers, and a squadron of scouts. The bomber pilots and the scout pilots all had the same training and flew the same types of planes—the Vindicator scout bomber or the Dauntless. The difference between a scout and a bomber was the mission assigned to the plane and the type of load it carried. A bomber carried a 1,000-pound bomb and about 50% less fuel than a scout. The scout would carry a 500-pound bomb; thus it could carry 100% more fuel than the bomber. The scouts' principal job was to search out the enemy and bomb if appropriate. The bomber's job was to deliver the ordinance after being directed by the Scout.

If the tactical situation required it, a carrier would launch a comprehensive 360-degree sea search for the enemy beginning at dawn. An imaginary circle of 200- to 250-mile radius was drawn around the carrier position. This circle was then divided into pie-shaped wedges, or sectors, about 10 degrees wide. It was a scout's job to search out a sector, flying at about 1,000 to 1,500 feet off the water to conserve fuel by avoiding a long climb to a higher altitude. Scouts were supposed to find the enemy and notify the carrier of the enemy's position. The report was sent by the gunner, in code if time permitted and in the clear if time was short. Only under very favorable conditions was a scout supposed to attack. Whenever possible, a scout flew into available cloud cover and stayed up-sun to avoid being spotted by the enemy combat air patrol fighters. Scouting was a boring job unless the pilot was successful in finding the enemy. Then it was very dangerous since the scout couldn't defend itself very well if the enemy CAP found him, which they frequently did.

One of the accidents often suffered in operational training and one that I witnessed was caused by pilots not being proficient in instrument flying. One night three of us were flying Vindicators and taking off on a moonless night for night flying practice with no horizon in sight. The first pilot took off and did not rely strictly on instruments. Vertigo overcame him and he crashed in a great ball of flame. The pilot behind him became too engrossed with the accident, and he, too, developed vertigo and spun in behind the first, also in a ball of flame. I was the third plane off and I didn't dare take my eyes away from that instrument panel!

When our final 200 training hours were over, we all had a party in a private room at the Pearl Harbor Officer's Club. It was a beautiful new club with the biggest bar I had ever seen, and there were gardens full of beautiful tropical flowers and trees. Most of us had dates, but some of the boys had their wives, whom they had married secretly since Navy rules stated that ensigns and second lieutenants were to be single. We danced and drank far into the night.

Training was over, or so I thought. I felt I was the red-hottest, toughest, best trained pilot in the Navy, which I thought was certainly better than the Marines—no matter what they thought; and we didn't even recognize Army pilots. I couldn't see why every girl in the country wouldn't fall for me the minute she laid eyes on me. I'm sure I was obnoxious.

The next day I got my orders to Pearl Harbor Air Station where I was to join a new carrier air group being formed. It was December 1,1941.

Pearl Harbor Naval Shipyard and Ford Island Naval Air Station, Oahu, Hawaii, May 2, 1940. (Courtesy Hawaiian Aviation Archives)

ELEVEN

Shore Patrol: Honolulu

S HORTLY AFTER BEING COMMISSIONED, I WAS SUMMONED to a conference with the executive officer of Pearl Harbor Naval Air Station. He informed me that as a junior ensign attached to that command, I was expected to perform Shore Patrol duty every other weekend for six months or until I was assigned to another activity. He explained that since I was new to the Navy, I would attend a two-day briefing on the duties of a Shore Patrol officer, which would begin the following Saturday.

The Shore Patrol is the military police organization of the Navy. U.S. military personnel are subject to military criminal law when actually on military reservations, facilities, or ships. However, when involved in misdemeanors and felonies while in civilian territory, they may be detained by civilian police, but must be turned over to military establishment for trial and punishment. In order to police its personnel in foreign ports, the ship assigns an appropriate detachment of men to police the liberty areas, thus the name, Shore Patrol.

In large ports which are frequently visited by American war ships or which have permanent naval bases, a professional Shore Patrol group is a part of the shore establishment. Honolulu was such a port. The permanent Shore Patrol organization required augmentation when large numbers of men came ashore all at once. Honolulu was regularly filled with sailors on weekends and that is why I became involved. For the most part, Shore Patrol duty in Honolulu came down to arresting drunks who were causing trouble, stopping fights, and searching brothels for the AWOLs and deserters who used them as hideouts. Most of these tasks could be handled by two or three SP's. However, once in a while, a drunken gang of sailors ransacked a brothel, tore up a bar, or attacked a gang of soldiers. Quelling such melees required large contingents of SPs, which frequently had to be reinforced by Army Military Police (MPs).

The worst and most dangerous occurrences were the dangerous knife fights in which someone was often killed. Usually, however, these occurred at night in a hidden spot in some blind alley, unseen by anyone except the participants settling a dispute. Frequent victims in these disputes were homosexuals and Filipinos, especially if they were foolish enough to be in a place populated by soldiers or sailors and display any money. Every weekend, two or three bodies were discovered somewhere in the myriad alleys in the red light district.

In 1941, the typical enlisted sailor or soldier was a product of the great Depression of the 1930s. He was the professional who was in the service for a twenty-year hitch because he couldn't get any other employment. Frequently he was illiterate, or close to it, and usually unmarried. He was rough and tough and probably had contracted venereal disease sometime during his service. His recreation was generally whoring, drinking, and bar fighting. He often carried a switchblade and knew how to use it. Depending on his rank and length of time in service, his pay varied from twenty-five to forty dollars a month, plus keep. He lived from payday to payday; in between, he stayed on base, played cards, and gambled.

In those days, the difference between officers and enlisted men was the difference between royalty and peasants. Officers were generally educated in one of the service academies, or a civilian equivalent, and were considered "gentlemen." They were relatively highly paid, wore tailor-made clothing, and lived in nice quarters in which no enlisted men were permitted, except when assigned to officers as servants. Officers had no social contact whatsoever with enlisted personnel. If they violated this dictum, they were ostracized by their peers, and their career in the service was ruined. Any friendship or camaraderie between officers and enlisted men occurred strictly during working hours, and then it really didn't occur often, except under combat conditions when lives depended upon it. Generally, enlisted men disliked officers immensely, and most officers didn't care. In fact, they expected to be unpopular.

Honolulu Shore Patrol headquarters was on King Street near the jail. As ordered, I reported there for Shore Patrol indoctrination the following Saturday morning. I was interviewed by a lieutenant commander who invited me to coffee and explained the system. In the city, the Shore Patrol was on duty twenty-four hours a day, every day. Two officers were always on duty in the office: a senior lieutenant and an ensign, or junior grade lieutenant, as well as several chief petty officers. The officers didn't patrol; they were expected to stay in the office and administer the operation. However, in case of very serious problems such as a homicide, one of them had to go to the scene because an officer was required to testify at the coroner's inquest. Otherwise, a chief petty officer (CPO) could handle most everything. Officers and CPOs were the only Shore Patrol authorized to carry hand guns and were required to do so when on duty. All Shore Patrol personnel wore working uniforms with arm brassards marked with a big SP. In addition, the patrolmen wore whitewashed canvas leggings.

After the Lieutenant Commander had enumerated the SP officer's basic duties, we shook hands and he said he'd introduce me to Chief Petty Officer Zimmerman, who would go further into detail. Zimmerman was a burly man of about thirty-five and had narrow shoulders, pussy hips, and a paunch—not the typical SP type who was preferably over 200 pounds, athletic and brawny. As it turned out, he knew the police business cold. He'd been a shore patrolman for fifteen years, much of it in Honolulu. He said his instruction would consist of a brief review of military law, weapon handling, personal defense, and a walk through the red light district to show me the territory.

He explained that on weekends and paydays literally thousands of sailors and soldiers crowded this part of town, the center of which was Hotel Street. Hotel Street ran about a mile along the waterfront and connected to myriad side streets and winding alleys, some blind and some leading to Beretania Street to the east or to King Street to the west. Zimmerman estimated that within this small area, which covered no more than half a square mile, there were over a hundred bars and fifty brothels of one kind or another.

We spent Saturday afternoon discussing subjects such as the power and prerogatives of the military police in general, the relationship of military police with civilian police, and army military police. Generally the organizations left one another's people alone unless the situation was too large to handle; then they could ask the other organizations for help. The Shore Patrol could arrest soldiers, and vice versa; however, the soldiers must be turned directly over to their own police as soon as possible. Such steps were to be taken only in special situations, such as stopping fights where servicemen from more than one service were involved.

The session on weapons was short. I already knew how to handle and shoot a Colt 45, a cutoff shotgun, and a Springfield rifle. Self defense was something else. Instruction started the next morning. Zimmerman made no attempt to teach physical combat in half a day, but explained and demonstrated what I could absorb in a short time.

First he advised me that a uniformed officer, military policeman or not, should never, armed or unarmed, walk alone into a bar or a brothel where there could or would be enlisted men drinking. If he did, there was a good chance he'd be in more trouble than he could handle. "Some drunk with a knife will be an officer hater," he explained. For the same reason, Shore Patrol officers in uniform should never go anywhere without two armed guards carrying riot guns, and, if possible, all be riding in a jeep. When walking the streets, Shore Patrol enlisted men always patrolled in pairs and entered bars only when covered by a second pair of SPs standing at the door. Since the chief had mentioned knife fighting several times, I was very curious. "How about showing me something about knife fighting?" I asked.

"Mr. McCandless, officers don't fight with knives. If anyone ever pulls a knife on you, back off and pull your gun. That's what it's for. Give a quick warning once; then shoot to kill. That's standard practice with all military police," he explained.

"What if I don't have a gun?" I queried.

"Then run. If you can't run, pick up a chair and keep it in front of you, but somehow get away. You don't have a choice. Anybody carrying a knife who's drunk and an officer-hater, will use it," Zimmerman responded.

"Show me anyway, Chief," I appealed.

"Okay. For one thing, it's only in the movies that a knife fighter will stab and miss, slash and miss, and tussle over several city blocks. Figure one offensive thrust-and-miss, and maybe two if you're lucky. Most knife fighters are counter-punchers, so it's all over in thirty seconds or so. The guy that gets stuck first usually ends up getting his throat cut. Dead men tell no tales, particularly if there are no witnesses, and somehow there never are," he said with a knowing look.

Zimmerman went over to a desk and took a knife from the drawer. It was a brass-bound clasp knife with a five-inch snap-button blade and walnut handles that ended in little hand guards between which the blade passed as it closed. I pushed the button, and the blade snapped out. I closed the knife and handed it back to him. He took the knife, snapped it open, and took the classic stance of a practiced knife fighter: crouched slightly, right arm out a little, blade held sharp edge down projecting from across the upturned palm between the thumb and index finger, left arm up as a guard, the knife waving slowly back and forth like a snake head.

"This is the stance. Stand on the balls of your feet. Here's the knife. Take the position. Now lunge like you were fencing." We went on like this for about five minutes. Then he said, "Enough. Now you know how dangerous this can be; just don't ever try it. One other thing, if you stick a man in the kidney with a knife, it hurts so bad he can't make a sound. That's the way you get a guard or a sentry from behind. Also, remember to use your gun fast if you're ever attacked. Some of these bastards will throw the knife when you go after the gun."

After some discussion about the techniques used in quelling fights and riots, we adjourned for lunch. On the way out, Chief Petty Officer Zimmerman saluted me and said he'd meet me here in an hour, and we'd tour the Shore Patrol district to which I'd been assigned. Being an officer, and in accord with Navy protocol, I had a Navy automobile and driver transport me to Trader Vic's, where I had lunch while the driver waited outside.

Fat Sam, the head waiter, seated me in my favorite corner and I ordered lunch. While I was waiting, I sipped a Mai Tai and contemplated the whole situation. Up to now the Navy was peaches and cream—great camaraderie, flying airplanes all day (my favorite pastime), and dancing every weekend at fine hotels with lovely young socialites. But this Shore Patrol business was a sordid, brutal, filthy thing. Even my instructor confided to me that he was getting a shot every two weeks for syphilis that he'd contracted several years ago. By the time my food was served, I'd decided that I was simply beginning to see the real world and was feeling the pangs of culture shock. I was right about that. What I didn't know was that the culture shock had hardly started.

When I returned, Zimmerman was waiting with a Shore Patrol jeep, complete with two armed guards. The chief explained the tour. We would start walking at the Army-Navy Y.M.C.A., across from Palace Square facing King Street, then up Punch Bowl Street to Hotel Street, which anchored the south end of the district. We would then proceed north about a mile, to the point where King angles into Hotel Street across the river at Aala Park, which marked the north end of the district. Then we would cut east up River Street to Beretania Street, and return to the Y.M.C.A. via the spider web of side streets and alleys between Beretania and Hotel Street. The Y.M.C.A. was a big, rambling, three-story building which sat in the middle of a huge grass lawn and was camouflaged by palm trees. Directly in front of it on King Street was a cab stand for all the Fort Schofield and Pearl Harbor taxies. Kitty-corner, across the street from the cab stand, was the Black Cat Cafe, where everybody got that first "best-drink" upon arriving and his last and "worst-drink" when departing. The Black Cat was open-fronted with a long bar to better accommodate the big line of servicemen pushing and shoving to get served. We kept on walking to crowded Hotel Street, which was lined on both sides by one and two-story frame buildings. We threaded our way through groups of sailors and soldiers who rolled along drunkenly, arm-in-arm, and hissing-footed Filipinos, padding along femininely in twos and threes (but never single) in their wide-shouldered zoot suits. The store fronts offered everything a serviceman on leave could want: bars, liquor stores, restaurants, tattoo shops, shooting galleries, photo shops, pawn shops, clothing stores, and an unending number of souvenir shops—all run by Chinese. In between every two or three store fronts were the dark stairs leading to the second floor and the waiting prostitutes. Eternally, everywhere, pervading everything like fate, was the smell of rotting meat and dead wilted vegetables from the open-fronted grocery stores. Every now and then whiffs of heavy, cheap, gardenia perfume wafted down from second-story windows. Smells I will never smell again without remembering the Honolulu tenderloin.

I told Zimmerman I wanted to examine a souvenir store, and shortly we came to Wufangs. It was one of those dingy little stores, exactly like a thousand other dingy little stores that exist wherever sailors and soldiers live or go on liberty. At Wufangs you could have your pants tailored and your shirts cut down. You could buy such things as chevrons, shooter's medals, garrison caps, solid brass insignia, brilliantly colored shoulder patches, whistles, ribbons, belt buckles, scarves, pillows with "Hawaii" or hula girls printed on them, and switchblades.

Our next stop was the Paradise Hotel. "I think you ought to see the best whore house in Honolulu," Zimmerman said. "I've been in the best there are, too: Amsterdam, Hamburg, Brussels, Shanghai, Hong Kong, and they ain't no better than here."

The Paradise Hotel was set back off Beretania Street in an alley, surrounded by stinking grocery stores and a couple of bars. We climbed the stairs and were confronted on the landing by a massive steel door with a square peephole. The door was covered with the graffiti of countless sailors and soldiers: naked bodies, unattached bodiless organs, and pornographic verse. One of our body guards beat on the door with the butt of his riot gun. The peephole slid back immediately and a huge black Hawaiian face peered out suspiciously.

"Shore Patrol. Open up!" Zimmerman commanded.

"We don't want no trouble with Shore Patrol. This is a respectable place. We closed," a voice from behind the door said.

"Tell Mrs. Lucas CPO Zimmerman is here to introduce a new officer. This ain't no search," he said.

The peephole closed for a minute; then opened again to reveal a pretty smiling white woman who said, "Well hello, Joe. Just a minute." There was a sound of steel rubbing steel and the door swung inward and the sophisticated-looking woman, perfectly groomed with an excellent figure daintily encased in an evening gown decorated with a corsage, said, "Please come in. Introduce me to your friend."

Zimmerman introduced me and stepped out of the way.

"Pleased to meet you Mr. McCandless. Let me show you around," Mrs. Lucas said.

"Nice to meet you, Mrs. Lucas," I answered.

The entry room opened into a large waiting room, well furnished with overstuffed furniture. In the corner a woman played the Wurlitzer piano while a couple of sailors leaned on it and watched. Around the room, several soldiers, sailors, and Marines were lounging on the sofas with girls dressed in long see-through gowns equipped with full length zippers.

"Mr. McCandless," Mrs. Lucas said earnestly, "this is a high-class legitimate entertainment center. I don't permit liquor of any kind on the premises, nor do I admit anyone who has been drinking. Business and drinking don't mix. I admit we've had to call the military policy to stop fights, but very rarely. Now, would you like to meet some girls? We just received some nice Caucasians from the States."

"No, Mrs. Lucas, this is strictly Navy business," I replied.

Accompanied by my guards, I inspected further and discovered there were several more waiting rooms, each occupied by men and girls. There was a very long hallway with doors on both sides, and every few minutes a girl, leading a man, would emerge from or disappear into one of the rooms. Some of the girls were gum-chewing cows who obviously did business only during the big "payday attack," but some were very comely. There were the Chinese girls with the flat side-view, but slender and curvaceous front-view; the Japanese girls, stockier with fuller figures; the Hapa-Portuguese girls with their hot, sultry sexiness; and the very white Caucasians who, by contrast, had to stay out of the sun. The house charged two dollars for native girls and three dollars for Caucasians

"It's time to leave," I told Zimmerman, and we left the Paradise Hotel.

That was my first and last visit to a brothel—more culture shock. We proceeded back to the jeep parked at the Y.M.C.A.

****

After a couple of weekends, I had the Shore Patrol job pretty well in hand. The duty watches were eight hours on and eight hours off for forty-eight hours. Being the most junior officer, I always got the 8:00 p.m. Friday to 4:00 a.m. Saturday watch, by far the most active period of the entire weekend. On Friday nights the enlisted men flooded our duty area like great herds of animals. By 4:00 a.m. most of them were drunk and broke. It was, to me, an earthy, sordid, depressing experience. I would never make a good cop or social worker.

Most of the time I spent at headquarters: ordering drunks to the brig, answering phone calls reporting fights, and dispatching the paddy wagon. However, I did have to inspect several homicides, which were the result of knife fights, and one murder of a prostitute who'd been choked to death by a sailor. I also handled two suicides: one in which a sailor hanged himself; the other, in which a sailor slashed his wrists. In all cases, I had to testify at the court inquest, which was irritating because it cost me good flying time.

One Saturday morning at about 1:00 a.m., two Army MPs and a first lieutenant dragged a semi-conscious sailor into Shore Patrol headquarters and dropped him on the floor. The officer was furious. "This man single-handedly tore up the Blue Anchor Cafe (a bar habituated almost entirely by Army enlisted men). He was hitting soldiers with a bottle. He's dead drunk, and I want him court-martialed. I'm charging him with attempted homicide!"

"Isn't that a pretty stiff charge for something that happens almost every day, Lieutenant?" I asked.

"God damn it! Do as I say!" he ordered.

"Yes, Sir," I replied as I saluted. Then the MPs left.

After calling for a doctor or an experienced medical corpsman to come to headquarters and examine the man's injuries, I turned him over to examine him myself. I knew him well. He was Airman 1st Class Andy Sonnenberg, the man in charge of maintaining and scheduling the N3N training planes at Pearl Harbor Naval Air Station. Anytime anyone wanted to fly an N3N, he had to schedule and be checked out in one by Andy. I frequently flew one on weekends myself. I'd call Andy on Friday, and

Saturday morning an N3N would be serviced and waiting for me. Sonnenburg was a fine man, I thought. When the medical corpsman, a chief petty officer, arrived, he immediately got to work.

After examining Sonnenberg, the chief said, "How did he get hurt?" I told him the story.

"Hell," he said, "this guy isn't in this condition entirely because of liquor. He's had the hell beat out of him by those MP's. I've seen this too many times. See all those head bruises without broken skin? That's done with those billy clubs. They also broke his nose. I'll bet they pounded on his kidneys too. I'd better get him to the infirmary."

"That's fine with me," I said.

"If he looks all right after you patch him up, I'd appreciate your getting him back to his barracks," I told the chief.

Apparently Sonnenberg heard and understood the conversation because he looked at me groggily and muttered, "Thank you, sir," as we lifted him into the back of the van.

The chief climbed in beside the driver and said in parting, "He'll be okay, sir; I'll take care of it." He saluted and they drove away.

I went back to check the prophylactic station the Navy kept to service sailors before and after their visits to the brothels. The whole thing was disgusting. It had been a long night, and I would be glad to get off duty. The next day I got a phone call from Sonnenberg. "I want to thank you, Mr. McCandless, for saving my ass."

"Are you all right?" I asked.

"Just a broken nose and a lot of sore spots. The chief medic sent me home last night," he explained.

"Good! Glad you're okay," I said. "Stay away from soldiers."

"Yes, Sir. I will. Good-bye, Sir."

TWELVE

Liberty

FLYING FIVE DAYS A WEEK AND DOING SHORE PATROL every other weekend was a grueling schedule, leaving only two weekends a month for recreation. After I was commissioned, I found it necessary to give up my quarters at the Makiki because it was an hour's drive from the field and we usually started flying at 0730. Besides, there were briefings, ground school, and night flying which fouled up the daily routine. Accordingly, I moved to the bachelor officers' quarters at Ewa Marine Air Station. I shared a room with a flight surgeon, which was a good deal because he kept me supplied with 180 proof grain alcohol that was good for making Hawaiian punch and other drinks at parties.

On Friday afternoon of the free weekends, I dressed in civilian clothes, packed a garment bag with Palm Beach suit or white tuxedo and accessories including alcohol, and headed for my friends' quarters at the Makiki Hotel. We usually partied on Friday and Saturday night and went to the beach during the day, but frequently we went hotel dancing or were invited to private luaus. In fact the Makiki had what we now call a barbecue area, where we gave a few luaus ourselves. By now we all had little black books with names and phone numbers of acceptable and available girls, who were getting harder and harder to find because of the military as well

as civilian population build-up occurring in Honolulu. However, we had a
head start and no really serious problems on that score. None of us had any
regular girls. We just played the field.

One weekend in October a ship needed emergency repairs and Steve and
Larry, my friends who were Naval architects in the Construction Corps
stationed at Pearl Harbor Ship Yard, had to work. They told me that I'd have
to make my own weekend plans, but I could stay at their Makiki apartment
as usual. Having made no previous arrangements for a date, I got on the
phone with my little black book for reference, but it was too late. I'd have
to find company some other way.

I packed the white Palm Beach suit and made a reservation for an early
dinner at Trader Vic's, hoping I might find some company, but I had no
luck there. After dining I went on to Lau Ye Chai's and had a drink at the
bar, but saw nobody I knew there, either. I knew I really couldn't expect to
find a date. In those days, "nice" girls didn't go out to restaurants or places
of entertainment unescorted, and after Shore Patrol experience, I was pretty
choosey, not that I wasn't before.

What I had hoped to do was to find a group of friends I could join, so I
went on to the Royal Hawaiian Hotel. I situated myself at the end of the bar
in the dinner ballroom. This was the best place for a single man to place
himself since everybody had to go around that end of the bar to get to the
restrooms. Sooner or later just about everybody in the ballroom would come
by. I nursed a martini and felt sorry for myself as I watched everybody
dancing—lots of good-looking girls.

I noticed one particularly nice-looking blond dancing with a burly looking
man. He was so drunk she was almost holding him up. I watched them go
to their table and saw her motion the waiter to go away, indicating she
wanted no more drinks at that table. I judged the burly-looking man to be a
little older than I. He was bobbing and weaving around even in his chair—
boy, was he fried! They missed the next dance, and as my martini took hold,
she gradually became unearthly beautiful. She had shoulder-length golden
hair, blue eyes, and a lovely slender figure encased in a white evening gown
with an orchid corsage at her shoulder.

I decided I'd better let up on drinking for a while since I had reached my
limit. I stayed at the bar, hoping she would go to the restroom. Sure enough,

she did. As she came by, I managed to make eye contact and say hello. I was surprised when she returned my smile. When she came back, I stood up and she hesitated. I asked her to dance. "Your friend won't care, will he?" I queried.

"I don't think we've been introduced," she said.

Does it matter?" I asked. "I'm only asking for a dance. I'll ask your friend."

"Yes, I'll dance," she answered. "You needn't talk to him. He won't know the difference."

The night was still young and the music was great. The Hawaiian songs and first floor show were over and the orchestra was now playing the old standard dancing songs of the 1930s: "It's June in January," "Night and Day," "Lost in a Fog," "Love Is Like A Cigarette," "All Of Me," and "Orchids In The Moonlight," etc.

We introduced ourselves. Her name was Winnifred Wilcox. She was from Richmond, Virginia, and had gone to Duke University. The man she was with was her brother-in-law, Clifford Brown, Annapolis, 1937, a naval aviator just back from three months at sea. His wife was in Richmond, Virginia, with her mother, and he had to go back to sea on Monday. That's why he had gotten drunk.

I looked over at him and his head was beginning to droop. After we had danced several numbers, I said, "Winnifred, I think we ought to put Brown in a chair in the lobby. Otherwise he'll be on or under the table."

"That's a good idea, but I'll try to take him in alone. I think he can walk and I don't want to make a scene," she said.

When she came back we danced for half an hour or so. Then I said, "Let's go out on the lanai and get some air."

"Only on one condition: no advances!" she replied. "You know very well I'm married."

"Yes, I noticed your rings," I responded. "Tell me about him." Suddenly she said, "You're a naval aviator."

"Yes, how did you know?" I asked.

"Because you're so damned confident and cocky. I can spot one anywhere—I married one!" she answered. "I really don't think I trust you."

"You really know how to hurt a guy," I said. "Let's go outside and I'll prove I'm clean-cut and trustworthy—just like the Annapolis boys." That hurt and she backed away, but I grabbed her hand. She didn't want a scene, so she let herself be led out.

It was a wonderful romantic Hawaiian night—cloudless and warm, with just enough breeze to blow her hair in little wisps. She told me that her husband was Annapolis, 1938, and a reconnaissance pilot on the cruiser *Chicago*, which always seemed to be at sea. They owned a house in the Alewa district. We talked some more.

Then I said, "What a beautiful night to fly." She agreed. "You're not afraid to fly at night?" I asked.

"No. I've even had flying lessons," she stated.

"Will you go if I can get a plane?" I asked.

"Sure, but where can you possibly get a plane at ten o'clock Friday night?" she asked.

"Let's go back in and I'll make a phone call," I said.

I called the first class petty officers' barracks at Pearl Harbor Naval Air Station and, with my fingers crossed, asked for Sonnenberg. He wasn't in the barracks, but he was on the station, probably at the movies. I called the movie theater and asked to have him paged.

In about five minutes he answered. He recognized my voice and asked, "Yes, Sir, Mr. McCandless, what can I do for you?"

"Andy, I want to check out an N3N," I answered.

"Isn't it awful late for that, Sir?"

"Well it is, but I want to go anyway." I'm sure he could hear music in the background even though I tried to cover the mouthpiece. "You're not breaking any regulation to let me have the plane at night, are you?" I asked.

"No, Sir. I just have to tell the tower it's Okay. Excuse me, Sir, but you're not drinking are you?"

"Yes, a little bit, but there's something else. I want to take a passenger."

"Sir, I'll fly the plane over to John Rogers Airport. The runway lights are on all night, but the tower shuts down at ten o'clock. That way nobody will ever know you had the plane."

"That's great! How about an hour from now?"

"Okay, Sir."

I went back to the table and proudly said, "Come on, Winnifred, I got a plane. Let's take Brown to your house. You can change your dress and get a jacket. You take him in your car, and I'll follow you. We meet the plane in an hour."

When we got to the airport, I saw the yellow N3N in front of the passenger terminal with the engine gently idling. There was nobody around except a couple of civilian guards who paid no attention to us when we walked out to the plane. Sonnenberg had thoughtfully brought two leather jackets and two pairs of goggles, which he handed us.

"Take your time, Sir. I'll be here." We both knew we were breaking all sorts of Navy regulations, but that we didn't discuss. I helped Winnifred get in the front, and I climbed in the back cockpit. The engine was warm, so off we went.

Rogers Airport was located on the beach west of Honolulu, just east of Pearl Harbor. I flew south, out to sea about half a mile or so and leveled off at about 1500 feet; then turned east, which took us along the Honolulu waterfront past the Aloha Tower, the boat harbor, and the hotel where we'd been dancing; then on to Diamond Head, where we made a 180-degree turn and retraced our route. The night was still beautiful and clear, except for the crown of clouds surrounding the mountain tops. The lights of Honolulu were sparkling like a huge waterfall spilling out of the clouds. I flew farther out to sea and higher to get a better view. Then I decided to go around the island. I didn't cut across Oahu anywhere because of the clouds.

It was a ball, flying in that open cockpit plane, the warm wind in our faces, the smooth steady hum of the engine, and the white surf with lights from the waterfront houses marking the shore. "Are you all right?" I shouted through the speaking tube. I got no answer, then remembered that she didn't know how to use the speaking tube. We flew up the waterfront on the final stretch at about 1:00 a.m. and the lights of the waterfall had thinned out—a sleeping city.

When I landed, Sonnenberg was waiting. He grinned when I shook his hand and said, "Thanks. You took a chance getting the plane for me. I hope you won't have any trouble when you land back at the base."

"No problem, Sir. You took a much bigger chance helping me."

The USS *West Virginia*, USS *Tennessee*, and USS *Arizona* during the Pearl Harbor attack, 7 Dec 1941. (Courtesy Franklin D. Roosevelt Presidential Library and Museum)

THIRTEEN

Pearl Harbor

ON MONDAY, DECEMBER 1, I HAD BEEN TRANSFERRED from Ewa to a small group of Airedales (aviators) at the Pear Harbor Naval Air Station BOQ (bachelor officer quarters), waiting to be assigned to a carrier squadron as a replacement or to a new air group being formed. Since I was a civil engineer, I was assigned temporary duty with the NAS Public Works Department to handle odd jobs until my assignment came through. After work I could usually get an airplane for an hour or two to shoot landings and keep current. On Friday, December 5, I found I'd been scheduled to stand the forenoon watch (0800 to 1200) on Sunday, December 7. My duty was to be the Junior Officer of the Day at the air station headquarters building. This duty assignment shortened my weekend, but I could still follow my usual routine of going to my friends' apartment at the Makiki Hotel. At least I could get in a Friday and Saturday night; then go back to the base early Sunday morning. I put on civilian clothes, took the 1730 boat from Ford Island across the channel to the parking lot at the Pearl Harbor Officer's Club, got my car, and drove to Honolulu. Steve and Larry arrived at about the same time I did, so we had a drink. Since we had no dates for the evening, we decided to "stag" it back at the officer's club at Pearl Harbor.

Saturday was a beautiful day. We went to the beach at the Blow Hole. That night we took dates to a private Luau given by a contractor who was doing a Navy job under the direction of the Public Works Department on Ford Island whom I'd met while acting as a navy inspector. The party was outstanding. The entertainment was lively with lots of hula girls, and there was plenty of cocktail time for drinking Mai Tais and daiquiris and eating pupu's (Hawaiian hors d'oeuvres) before the pig and sweet potatoes were served.

We got home sometime around 0200, and I slept for three hours. At 0500 on the morning of December 7, still feeling the Luau booze, I arose and drove to Pearl Harbor in time to catch the 0600 boat back to Ford Island.

****

At this point I should digress and explain that Ford Island sits in the middle of Pearl Harbor, is about a mile long and half as wide, and is roughly rectangular in shape with its long axis running southwest to northeast. Parallel to this axis, and very close to the southeast shoreline, lies battleship row: six ships aligned in pairs, end to end, with four more ships moored singly. Of these ten ships, seven were battleships. On the northwest shore, four smaller ships were similarly tied up. In addition, about fifty Navy ships were anchored around the harbor, including some in the ship yard's dry dock, across the channel.

Ford Island itself was the location of Pearl Harbor Naval Air Station, but the names Ford Island and Pearl Harbor were used interchangeably. The island could accommodate 250 or more planes which included flying boats, carrier air groups, and various land-type utility aircraft. It was complete with shops, hangars, warehouses, and living quarters for a couple of thousand men

****

As I walked along the southeasterly shore of Ford Island from the boat landing, to the old BOQ building located at the northeast quarter of the air station, I passed within 150 feet or so of the line of battle ships called "Battleship Row." First, I passed the *Maryland* and *Oklahoma*, next the *Tennessee* and *West Virginia*, then the *Arizona* and the repair ship, *Vestal*, which was sitting outboard of the *Arizona*. A little further beyond lay the battleship *Nevada*. When I was opposite the *Arizona*, I turned left and walked inland a couple of hundred feet into the BOQ.

By the time I got to my room, it was about 0630. I showered, shaved, put on a clean white uniform, then headed across the island for breakfast, which was being served at the new BOQ located at the northwest tip of the island. When I arrived at the dining room at about 0700, I found an excellent breakfast buffet laid out on a long linen-covered table, decorated with silver vases filled with Hawaiian flowers. There were pitchers of exotic juices and heated casseroles containing every kind of food one could imagine for breakfast. Since it was Sunday morning, virtually nobody else had appeared except for a couple of other officers going on duty. I ate my usual large breakfast of kippered herring, ham and eggs, fresh biscuits, juice, and about a half-gallon of coffee to wake me up and help rid myself of a slight hangover. While I was eating, a mess boy came over to me with a telephone message: The OD (Officer of the Day) sedan, which was to pick me up at 0745, would be late. I phoned back and told them not to send a car because I'd walk down to headquarters and, therefore, I might be a little late. On my way to headquarters, I decided to stop at my quarters in the old BOQ to get my white gloves which I'd forgotten. Along the walk between the BOQs, I was joined by another aviator whom I hadn't previously met.

As we approached the old BOQ at about 0745, we heard the drone of aircraft. We looked up to see twenty-five or thirty planes orbiting Pearl Harbor. They were quite high—probably 4,000-5,000 feet, I guessed, because we could barely see them even in the clear blue sky.

"Why is the stupid Army flying on Sunday?" my companion muttered.

"Who knows?" I replied.

A few moments later, we noticed a plane coming from the northeast, diving toward the south end of Ford Island. We had reached the old BOQ by now and were standing between it and the *Arizona*. Suddenly a great roar engulfed us—seemingly from all directions—as planes flying very low swept in from the east, passing low over our heads. A large red ball was painted on the under surface of their wings. My companion must have realized what was happening about the same time as I because we turned and looked at each other simultaneously with absolutely shocked expressions.I remember yelling at him that there were some of our Navy fighter planes on the north apron. Together we started running for the fighters; then the lights went out for me. I have never known what happened to my companion.

FOURTEEN

War

"In peace there is nothing so becomes a man as modest stillness and humility; but when the blast of war blows in our ears, then imitate the tiger; stiffen the sinews, summon up the blood..."
—Henry V, Act III, Scene i

IN WRITING ABOUT THE WAR FORTY YEARS LATER AND HAVING repressed these memories for most of this time, I find that in looking back through the lens of time we balkanize the past and find our recollections are as fragmented and jumbled as the jungles we toiled through. Moreover, the recollections of incidents, people, and places constantly distort, getting larger and smaller, clearer and dimmer. Sometimes I can't recall whether I actually did something, dreamed it, or read about it. But, of course, some recollections are so poignant they never die. I might add that getting a severe head concussion from a blast at Pearl Harbor probably hasn't helped my memory much either. Napoleon said that his soldiers' only view of Russia was the rear view of the men in front, and that's pretty much the case with me. It was only after reading many history books concerning the war that I was able to ascertain the significance of the actions of which I was a part. For example, I only remember the first three or four minutes of the surprise attack on Pearl Harbor, and it was long after the war that I learned the strategy that caused me to be stationed on Ulithi, Saipan, and all the others.

During the interval between my senior year in college and the outbreak of the war in the Pacific, I, like my friends and most Americans, was ignorant of any war-like threat from the Far East and only mildly concerned with the war in Europe. At Stanford the subject was simply not discussed. No one seemed to know or care—at least not in my circle of friends.

I first heard Hitler over a portable radio while working on the surveying crew during the summer of 1939. We were eating lunch on the hillside construction site of the Permanente Cement Plant, and Hitler was yelling and screaming in German, while an interpreter was trying to keep up with him in English. He was announcing Germany's military invasion of Poland. It was this action, of course, that caused England and France to declare war the next day.

The surveying crew's only reaction to that speech, as I recall, was that Bud Cameron, our survey party chief and classmate, told us that we had better buy sugar because there would be a shortage of it if there were a war in Europe. Bud was several years older than we were because he'd worked four years before he went to college; so we considered him an authority on everything. We all went to the store that night and bought sugar and gave the rest of the affair no more thought, not even when Bud quit his job two weeks later and joined the Army.

However, as the months went by, the United States government and newspapers became more and more concerned with the war in Europe, but still paid little attention to the Japanese sun rising in the east. Later, when General Courtney Hodges captured the Remagan Bridge over the Rhine River, Bud Cameron, then Colonel Cameron, United States Engineers, 1st Army, joined the attack on the bridge and defused the explosives the Germans had placed there to blow it up. He thereby helped capture the first bridge over the Rhine for our invading armies.*

---

* In 1979 I met Bud at our fortieth Stanford class reunion. He said he'd gotten a direct commission as a second lieutenant in the Corps of Engineers. After training at Fort Belvoir, he was assigned to an engineer regiment which, under General George S. Patton, was the first into action at Casablanca in November 1942. He fought across Africa, Sicily, and the mainland of Italy. Later he made the Overlord landing at Normandy, crossed the Remagan Bridge over the Rhine, and saw the end of the war in Germany. After making a career in the Army, he retired a brigadier general with thirty years of service.

The vast majority of Americans were interested in events in Europe and were aware of European geography because they were descended from European immigrants. They also had studied European history and geography in school. When commentators told them the Nazi spearheads were knifing here and there, they needed no maps to visualize the terrain. They all had maps in their minds. Asian geography, on the other hand, was and still is a mystery to most Americans. Additionally, most Americans were not interested in the events in Asia.

The Japanese had been fighting in China since 1931. In 1937 the Japanese had bombed and sunk the U.S. gunboat Panay on the Yangtze River and jeered when the administration in Washington, shackled by isolationism, had done nothing. Even among those of us who call ourselves interventionists, Hitler was regarded as the true enemy. It was Hitler who Roosevelt had been trying to provoke with the Atlantic Charter to destroy our swap with Britain, Lend Lease and the shoot-on-sight convoys. Each of these acts drew Washington closer to London.

Europe, we thought, was where the danger lay. Roosevelt had never changed his priorities. However, when the Fuhrer refused to rise to the bait, the President found another way to lead us into the war, which he felt was absolutely essential if the next generation of Americans was to be spared a hopeless confrontation with a hostile totalitarian world.

On September 27, 1940, the Japanese signed the Tripartite Pact with Germany and Italy. That action opened the possibility of reaching the Axis through Tokyo, and Roosevelt knew how to do it. During the four months before the pact, the fall of France, Holland, and Belgium had wholly altered the strategic picture in Asia. European colonies were almost defenseless, but Roosevelt let it be known that he felt avuncular. Even before the Tripartite Pact, he had warned the Japanese to leave French Indo-China alone. Once the Japanese tilted toward the Axis, he proclaimed an embargo on scrap iron and steel to all the nations outside the western hemisphere, Great Britain excepted. He reached the point of no return in the summer of 1941. On July 24, the Japanese troops formally occupied Indo-China, including Vietnam. Two days later the President froze all Japanese credits in the United States, which meant no more oil from America. Britain followed suit. This situation was serious for the Japanese, but not desperate. Their chief source of petroleum was the Netherlands East Indies, now Indonesia, which sold them 1.8 million tons a year. Then came the real shock: the Dutch Colonial Government in Djakarta froze Japanese assets there and renounced its oil contract with Dai Nippon (*Dai* meaning Great; and *Nippon*, Japan).

For Fumimaro Konoye, Emperor Hirohito's premier, this was a real crises. Virtually every drum of gas and oil used for fueling the army's tanks and planes had to be imported. Worse, the Japanese navy, which until now had experienced no confrontations, consumed as much as 400 tons of oil an hour. The Japanese navy joined the army in calling for war. Without Dutch petroleum the country could hold out for only a few months, no more.

Konoye submitted his government's demand to the American Ambassador in Tokyo. If the United States would stop arming the Chinese, stop building new fortifications in the Pacific, and help the Emperor search for raw materials and markets, then Konoye promised not to use Indo-China as a base, to withdraw from China after the situation had been settled, and to guarantee the neutrality of the Philippines. Washington sent back an ultimatum: Japan must withdraw all troops from China and Indo-China, withdraw from the Tripartite Pact, and sign a non-aggression pact with neighboring countries. On October 16, Konoye, who had not been unreasonable, stepped down and was succeeded by General Tojo, who was known as the "Fiercest Hawk" in Asia. The embargoed Japanese believed that they had no choice. They had to go to war unless they left China, which was a loss of face and, therefore, unthinkable. They began honing their ceremonial Samurai swords.

All of this information was known in the Pennsylvania Avenue building that housed the State, War, and Navy Departments. There was only one question—Where would the Japanese attack? There were so many possibilities: Thailand, Hong Kong, Borneo, Guam, Wake, Indonesia, Malaysia, or the Philippines. Pearl Harbor had been ruled out because Tojo was known to be massing troops in Saigon, and American officers felt sure that these "myopic, banty-legged little yellow men" couldn't mount more than one offensive at a time. Actually, they were preparing to attack all of these objectives, including Pearl, simultaneously. In fact, the threat to Hawaii became clear in the last weeks of peace. FDR's chiefs of staff and U.S. Intelligence were in possession of the Japanese code and could follow every development in Dai Nippon's higher echelons.

On November 22, a message from Tokyo to its embassy on Washington's Massachusetts Avenue warned, "In a week, things are automatically going to happen." On November 27, referring to the possibility of war, the Emperor's envoy to the United States asked, "Does it seem as if a child will be born?" He was told, "Yes, the birth of a child seems imminent. It seems as if it will be a strong, healthy boy." Finally, on November 29, the United States Signal Corps transcribed a message in which a functionary at the Japanese Washington Embassy asked, "Tell me when Zero Hour is." The voice from Tokyo replied softly, "Zero hour is December 8, at Pearl Harbor." (December 7 in the United States).

The Americans now knew that an attack was coming, when it would occur, and where. The danger could hardly have been greater. Japan's fleet was more powerful in Pacific waters than the combined fleets of America and Great Britain. U.S. commanders in Hawaii and the Philippines were told, "This dispatch is to be considered a war warning. An aggressive act is expected by Japan within the next few days." That was followed on December 6 by, "Hostilities may ensue. Subversive activities may be expected." The ranking general in Honolulu concluded that the message about hostilities was a reference to Japanese civilians on Oahu. Therefore, he ordered all military aircraft lined up in the middle of their air strips where they could be more closely guarded and protected from a ground attack, never considering the possibility of attack by enemy aircraft. This action, of course, made the military aircraft highly visible from the air and left them completely unprotected from air attack which could instantly destroyed them. The ranking admiral decided to take no other precautions. Put on constant alert, he felt his men would become exhausted.

Therefore, on December 6, officers and men were given their customary Saturday night liberty, and no special guards were mounted on the United States Fleet in Pearl Harbor—ninety-four ships, including seven commissioned battle ships and nine cruisers. The only force in being was to prevent new Japanese aggression in Asia. Of the Navy's 780 anti-aircraft guns in the harbor, only nineteen were manned, and of the Army's thirty anti-aircraft batteries, only four were manned. Most of them lacked any ammunition at all. It had been returned to storage because it was apt to get dusty.

In the early morning hours of Sunday, December 7, 1941, as Americans slept in Waikiki amid the scent of frangipani, the squawk of pet parrots, and the echo of the surf on Diamond Head, 200 miles north of them a mighty Japanese armada—thirty-one pagoda-masted warships—steamed southward at flank speed. The thoughts and prayers of all their crews were focused on the 360 carrier-borne war planes, especially those of the lead attack squadron aboard the flattop *Akagi*, followed by the *Soryu*.

In the darkness, the pilots scrambled across the flight decks to their waiting Nakajima bombers, Aichi dive bombers, and Kaga and Mitsubishi 0-type fighters. These latter were the swift lethal raiders Americans would soon call "Zeros." Zooming away, they approached Kahuku Point, the northern tip of Oahu, and howled through Kolekole Pass, which overlooked the U.S Army Schofield Barracks thirty-five miles from Honolulu. The squadron leader was told that if he found that he took the enemy by surprise, he was to break radio silence over Oahu and send back the code word *Tora*, Japanese for "tiger."

Luck rode with them. An overcast cleared and the sun appeared in a rosy satin dawn, sending warm pencils of light shining down upon green valleys and green-brown cane breaks, the purplish spiny mountain ridges, and the brilliant blue sea rimmed by valances of white caps. Dead ahead, on Oahu's southern coast, lay their targets: Ford Island, Kaneohe, Wheeler, Bellows, Ewa, and Hickam airfields and Pearl Harbor. There, off Ford Island in the center of the harbor, anchored in groups of two, lay the American battle wagons: the *California, Maryland, Oklahoma, Tennessee, West Virginia, Arizona, Nevada*, and the thirty-three year old *Utah*—then retired from active service.

From the Japanese height of 10,000 feet, the ships looked like toy boats in a bathtub swinging their chains around them, making escape almost impossible. Even if the "Men of War" could maneuver around the other eighty-six vessels which were concentrated in an area no more than three miles square, a torpedo net barred the one channel to the sea and freedom. The Japanese commander signaled his squadron, "*To, To, To!*" (the first syllable of *totsugeki*, meaning "charge"). He signaled the Flag Ship Akagi, "*Tora, Tora, Tora!*" (Tiger, Tiger, Tiger. We have surprised the enemy!) He then signaled his air fleet, "*Yoi!*" (Ready!) and "*Te!*" (Fire!) Flying at treetop level and defying the pitifully few dark grey bursts of flack polka-a-dotting the serene sky, successive waves of Japanese aircraft skimmed over Merry Point, attacking and wheeling, returning again and again. Zeros strafed, dive bombers and torpedo bombers dropped missiles and bombs through the rolling, reeking, oily clouds of smoke. The Japanese knocked out 347 U.S. war planes and eighteen warships, including all the battleships, the cruisers *Helena* and *Honolulu*, and the destroyers *Cassin* and *Downes*. It cost twenty-nine planes. The Japanese killed or wounded 3,581 Americans—nearly half of them in the sunken *Arizona*.

The destruction of the *Arizona*, which had been moored in tandem with the repair ship *Vestal*, was the most spectacular loss. A bomb set off fuel tanks which ignited eight tons of highly volatile black powder, stored against regulations. That, in turn, touched off vast stocks of smokeless powder in a forward magazine before it could be flooded. An instant later, three more bombs hit the *Arizona*, including one right down the funnel. The 32,600-ton battle wagon sent up a cascade of flames 500 feet high, leapt halfway out of the water, broke in two, and plunged to the bottom, her vanishing forecastle enshrouded in billowing smokes of black fumes. Over 1,000 Blue Jackets were incinerated or drowned. The time was 0759 hours, December 7,1941.

Not even the ancient Hawaiian war god, Kukailimoku, had envisioned such a disaster. "Remember Pearl Harbor!" became an American shibboleth and the title of one of the country's most popular war songs; however, it was the loss of the great ship *Arizona* that seared the minds of Navy men. Six months later at Midway, Naval Lieutenant Wilmer E. Galligher, Squadron Commander of U.S. Six (Scouting Six from the American carrier *Enterprise*) turned down the nose of his Dauntless dive bomber, roared almost 25,000 feet vertically, and released his 500-pound bomb onto the hull of the Japanese carrier *Kaga*, and blew her up. As Galligher pulled out at 2,500 feet he flicked on his radio and exalted, "*Arizona*, I remember you!"

The Japanese navy made several tactical mistakes when they attacked Pearl Harbor. The most obvious of these were: neglecting to destroy the Navy's huge fuel storage tanks located on the surrounding mountains; failing to attack the excellent ship repair facilities, which included dry-docks that could handle aircraft carriers and battleships; and failing to mount an amphibious attack on the Hawaiian Islands, which could have easily been conquered and occupied. The latter mistake is understandable since the Japanese hadn't dreamed the islands were so poorly defended by both the American Army and Navy.

The real miscalculation, though, was strategic—the effect of the attack on the morale of the United States. What had been a fractionated public— vocal isolationists, anti-war organizations, pro-war groups, neutralists, and a Congress representing all of these views—was now suddenly welded together and unanimously demanded that the United States go to war. They wanted immediate revenge.

The following is taken from an article in *Time Magazine* dated December 29, 1941:

> *Hello to Arms. Recruiting stations met the first rush by calling in additional clerks and doctors, keeping open twenty-four hours a day in some cities; sometimes staying open on Saturdays. But the wave of enlistments was no nine-day-wonder. Every time it receded, a new bulletin from the Pacific helped roll it up again. Good news or bad—either kind—made men want to join up. The Army signed up 10,646 men in the first week; the Navy, 11,303 men in eight days; the Marine Corps, an estimated 6,400 in ten days. Beyond that point recruiting office statisticians lost track, nor could any one count the additional thousands who had volunteered, but had not yet been accepted. There had never been*

anything like it—even in the most excited days of World War I—and for weeks young men and old stormed recruiting offices. In Los Angeles, Louis A. Tyler, forty-two, volunteered for the Navy to take the place of his son killed at Pearl Harbor. Dale W. Laughland, a one-man printing staff of the Worthington, Indiana Times, enlisted after setting a Navy recruiting advertisement. He left the paper temporarily unable to go to press. In Boston, Harold L. J. Sturdivant, kicked out of the Navy when he tore a swastika from the German Counselor's office in San Francisco last January, applied for reinstatement and got it. In Southbend, Indiana, a carnival worker, rejected by the Navy because he had a naked woman tattooed on his arm, reappeared the same afternoon with a woman dressed in skirt and brassiere. At the Greenville, North Carolina prison camp ten convicts volunteered for suicide squad duty. Said they, "Up to the present we have done no good deed for our country. Thus we have an indebtedness to the United States which must be removed." Most thorough-going volunteer was ranch-hand Harvey Penschulter of Hay Springs, Nebraska, who sold his horse and car for $500, put the money into defense bonds and then set out to join the Cavalry.

I was told that the *Arizona* blew up and caused an explosion and concussion wave so great that it blew out the fires on the burning ship, *Vestal*, next to her like an enormous candle snuffer and rained tons of debris—parts of the ship, legs, arms, and bodies—in a huge circle around her. I was found lying on the ground somewhere in this deluge and was taken to a make-shift field hospital set up in the Naval Air Station Marine barracks. Sometime that afternoon I regained consciousness. Since I could walk and talk and had suffered no visible wounds, I was released from the hospital. The small medical staff of one doctor and a few corpsmen and volunteers had, by this time, several hundred badly wounded and hideously burned men on their hands. About all the medics could do was administer a shot of morphine to each person and mark their foreheads with Mercurochrome to serve as an indication that they'd been attended to. I had a terrible headache, rather blurry vision, and some bruises but otherwise seemed all right. Actually, the first thing I recall was working that evening with a rescue party. I remember pulling oil-covered survivors out of the water. By that time, the bay around Ford Island swarmed with rescue activity amid constant explosions aboard ships, blazing oil floating on the water, and floating debris. Able-bodied survivors helped buddies off of burning battleships into launches, barges, and any other type of floating rig they could muster. The assorted craft plied back and forth from the hospital landing to Ford Island, picking men and bodies out of the water as they went.

Apparently, I wasn't of much use because a chief petty officer took me by the shoulders, looked into my eyes, and said softly, "You act like you're drunk, but I can tell you have a brain concussion. Go to your quarters and get to bed, and try to get an ice pack on your head. Tomorrow go to the hospital." Then he thoughtfully ordered one of his working party to lead me to my quarters and put me to bed.

The next day I reported to Pearl Harbor Naval Hospital located across the bay at the shipyard. An M.D. verified that I had a severe concussion. They put me to bed on a mattress on the floor in a hallway for a week and kept an ice pack on the left side on my head where it ached the worst. When the dilation of my eyes finally subsided, I was released and went back to the base where the flight surgeon cleared me for active duty.

FIFTEEN

The Battle of Midway

"But we in it shall be remembered—We few, we happy few, we band of brothers; for he today that sheds his blood with me shall be my brother; be he ne'er so vile this day shall gentle his condition…"
                                                                    —*Henry V,* Act IV, Scene iii

By any ordinary standard, they were hopelessly out-classed. They had no battleships, the enemy—eleven. They had eight cruisers, the enemy—twenty-three. They had three carriers (one of them crippled); the enemy had eight. The shore defense included guns from the turn of the century.

They knew little of war. None of the Navy pilots on one of their carriers had ever been in combat, nor had any of the Marine and Army pilots. Of the Marines, seventeen of twenty-one new pilots were just out of flight school—some with less than four hours flying time since then. Their enemy was brilliant, experienced, and all-conquering.

They were tired, dead tired. The patrol plane crews, for instance had been flying fifteen hours a day, servicing their own planes and getting perhaps three hours sleep at night. They had equipment problems. Some of the Marine land-based dive bombers couldn't dive—the fabric came off their wings. The Navy's torpedo planes were even worse. Yet they were up against the finest fighting planes in the world. They *took crushing losses—fifteen out of fifteen in one torpedo squadron, twenty-one out of twenty-seven in a group of fighters—many many more.*

They had no right to win. Yet they did, and in doing so they changed the course of the war. More than that, they added a new name—Midway—to that small list that inspires men by shining example. Like Marathon, the Armada, the Marne and a few others, Midway showed that once in a while "what must be" need not be at all. Even against the greatest of odds there is something in the human spirit, a magic blend of skill, faith, and valor, that can lift men from certain defeat to incredible victory."

—From *Incredible Victory* by Walter Lord

MOST MILITARY HISTORIANS AGREE THAT THE BATTLE of Midway marked the turning point in the war with Japan in the Pacific in favor of the United States. During the first five months the United States and her allies in the Pacific (England, France, Holland) had been on the losing end of practically every military or naval encounter. The Japanese seemed invincible. The morale and confidence of the Allied Forces was slipping, but the battle of Midway changed all this—at least as far as the United States was concerned. Midway Island, situated 1,136 miles northwest of Pearl Harbor, is the outermost link of the Hawaiian chain. It is made up of two islands in an atoll about six miles in diameter. Sand Island is less than two miles long, and Eastern Island is little more than a mile long. Midway had been an American possession since 1859 and has been a American naval air station since August 1941.

Strategically, the possession of Midway was of great value to both the United States and the Japanese. If the United States retained it, the U.S. could maintain a strong mid-Pacific airbase, which would help protect Hawaii as well as provide a base from which reconnaissance planes could cover a large part of the central Pacific. If Japan were to capture Midway, from which it could make land-based raids on Pearl Harbor and Honolulu, the invasion and occupation of Hawaii would become feasible. A Japanese-occupied Midway would guarantee Japan's security in the Pacific and possibly force President Roosevelt to the peace table.

In order to occupy Midway and go on to capture Hawaii, the Japanese first had to annihilate the American Pacific Fleet—hopefully in one big battle. Japan had already crippled the fleet at Pearl Harbor by disabling the battleships. Now it had to sink America's four aircraft carriers and what remained of the cruisers and destroyers.

To discuss in depth the detail and complexities of the battle of Midway is beyond the scope of this narrative. However, a brief description of the battle serves to explain and set the stage for my experience.

Basically, the Japanese battle plan at Midway was to lure the United States Navy into an unfavorable tactical situation, by cutting off its ability to retreat, driving in its flanks, then concentrating for the kill. They knew the Americans couldn't possibly match their naval force, which was far superior. It was a foregone conclusion, however, that the Americans would assemble their fleet and attempt to repel any invaders of American territory. It was also a foregone conclusion that the defenders of Midway Island were too weak to hold out even a day against an attack force of such overwhelming strength. However, the Americans knew well in advance of the Japanese plans to attack and also knew, to some degree, the Japanese order of battle, their strategy, and probable tactics. We were privy to this information because American naval intelligence had broken the Japanese top secret diplomatic codes "purple" as well as most of their naval codes.

On June 3, 1942, Admiral Yamamoto approached Midway from the northeast with four attack groups: 1) an advance force of submarines, 2) Admiral Nagumo's striking force (the one used at Pearl Harbor) which included four big carriers. 3) an occupation force of 5,000 solders on troop transports accompanied by a number of battleships, and 4) a main body of battleships and a carrier commanded by Admiral Yamamoto.

In addition to the attack force approaching Midway, a separate striking force was heading north to attack the American-owned Aleutian Islands near the Arctic Circle. The Aleutian attack was set up as a decoy to be accomplished before Midway was attacked and, hopefully, it would lure the American fleet away from Midway so it could be attacked without interference. The Japanese could trap and easily crush the inferior American fleet between the northern striking force, Admiral Nagumo's carrier force, and the main battle force. This plan assumed, of course, that the Americans had no knowledge of the Japanese plans and of Yamamoto 162 warships, which were then on their way to Midway.

Meanwhile, Admiral Nimitz, knowing the plan, set his own trap. He assembled all the warships he could: a total of seventy-six, including three big carriers—the *Enterprise, Yorktown*, and *Hornet*, but he had no battleships. The U.S. warships secretly approached Midway from the east and took initial positions northwest of the island, just beyond the search range of the approaching enemy planes. Admiral Nimitz anticipated that the 800-mile range of the search planes from Midway Island would locate the Japanese strike force before its planes discovered the waiting American fleet. Midway Island was defended by the Marine Sixth Defense Battalion, consisting of 750 men and a small land-based air force, which included sixteen PBY Navy reconnaissance flying boats, twenty-one high-level Army bombers, and seventy Marine and Navy carrier-type planes, mostly flown by Marines.

When one realizes that the Army Air Force B-17 Flying fortresses were designed to fly at high altitudes and bomb targets encompassing relatively large areas without pinpoint accuracy, it becomes obvious that they were not suited to effectively bomb ships. Of the Navy combat types, the thirty-eight Buffalo fighters and Vindicator dive bombers were obsolete death traps when facing state-of-the-art air opposition. Thus, the Marines on Midway were left with only thirty-two planes (Wildcats and Dauntlesses) which could put up a reasonable fight on a one-to-one basis. They faced an armada of excellent Japanese planes flown by seasoned pilots. Furthermore, there were only 800 ground defenders on Midway and 3,000 attackers. Midway was defenseless. All through the nights of June 3 and 4, unknown to both the Japanese and the defenders of Midway, the two opposing carrier forces approached each other at sea. At 0600 on June 4, the American fleet received a coded message from the Midway-based flying boat search planes. They had located the Japanese fleet. Immediately the American fleet carriers started launching their attack planes against the Japanese jugular vein—Admiral Nagumo's four carriers which were about two and one-half hours away to the west. At about the same time (0600 June 4th) the Japanese carriers launched 108 attack planes bound for the island of Midway. This force was about evenly divided among fighters, dive bombers, and level bombers. When the enemy was picked up on Midway radar at ninety-three miles out, twenty-eight Marine fighters scrambled to intercept them. Upon meeting the enemy, fifteen American planes and pilots were immediately lost to the deadly Japanese Zeros—but not without a fight. Between the combat air patrol and anti-aircraft fire, thirty-six Japanese planes were lost, but Midway Island received a devastating bombing.

An hour after the bombing, American bombers, including the ineffective Army Flying Fortresses and two flights of Marine dive bombers with sixteen Dauntlesses and eleven Vindicators, took off from Midway in an all-out attack on the enemy carriers. By necessity they had no fighter escort since most of the remaining thirteen Marine fighters needed repairs and had to provide combat air patrol for Midway. All planes found the target, but between the enemy's combat air patrol planes and the ships' anti-aircraft fire, fifteen Marine planes were immediately shot down. No damage was done to the enemy. The Army, flying B-17s at 20,000 feet, hit nothing and returned undamaged, but made great claims.

Now came the most critical part of the battle. At 0835 (June 4th), out of ammunition and nearly out of fuel, the planes of the Japanese carrier force that had struck Midway returned to their ships and began to land. At that moment the American strike force from the carriers *Enterprise, Hornet,* and *Yorktown* arrived and attacked—sinking all four Japanese carriers (the *Hiruyu, Soryo, Akagi* and *Kaga*) in about six minutes. All of this damage was inflicted by eighty-four Dauntless dive bombers. One-hundred percent of the attacking Japanese Naval Air Force was then effectively destroyed, since the planes and crews either sank with their ships or had no place to land and ditched into the ocean when they ran out of fuel.

American losses were heavy. Out of the forty-one American torpedo planes that attacked, only six survived. By now, the morning of the June 4, the American carrier *Yorktown* had been discovered by the enemy. Before the Japanese carrier *Hiru* was sunk, she sent her air group to attack the Yorktown and was successful in sinking her. Although the *Yorktown* was lost, most of her crew and planes were recovered aboard other American carriers. Besides losing the carrier *Yorktown*, the battle cost the U.S. 307 air crewmen and 147 aircraft. Unfortunately, the lost air crewmen included many our most experienced and best-trained men.

Overall, the battle was an absolute disaster for the Japanese fleet, which lost a total of four aircraft carriers, two heavy cruisers, 3,000 men and 234 aircraft, including the finest and most experienced pilots in her navy.

****

I arrived at Midway on May 30, 1942 in company with the Ford Island replacement squadron.and two other naval aviators who were fresh from flying school. We were delivered in a PBY, which flew the route daily hauling men and supplies. As soon as I arrived at Sand Island, I was billeted and reported to Commander Logan Ramsey. He was in charge of Naval Air Operations, which consisted principally of long-range patrolling with the twin-engine PBY flying boats, and immediately assigned me duty as a co-pilot on one of his PBYs scheduled to go on patrol the next morning. He looked surprised when I explained to him that I wasn't a multi-engine pilot. "You're supposed to be a reconnaissance pilot, McCandless," he said.

"Sir, I am, but I trained as a carrier scout—dive bomber type." I explained.

"All right, then the Marines can use you. Come to my briefing after dinner and I'll have you transferred," he replied.

I went to my quarters, took a shower, changed clothes, had dinner at the officers' mess, then sauntered to the briefing shack where forty or fifty men were assembling. Up to this point, I had no idea what was occurring with regard to the strategic plans involving Midway, which were being enacted at sea that very moment. The briefing officer was indeed brief and to the point.

"Gentlemen," he began. "We can expect a major air and sea attack on Midway in three or four days. Tonight at midnight we'll be at general quarters (general quarters, in Navy terminology, means all hands are standing at battle stations on full alert and ready for combat) until the attack is over."

The rest of the audience was obviously no better informed than I was, for we all stared straight ahead with startled looks on our faces. The looks were there for only a fleeting second before we began looking around at each other and talking under our breath excitedly. "Attention!" shouted the briefing officer. "Dismissed." The briefing was over.

The next morning I was transferred to the Marines on Eastern Island where I reported to Colonel Ira L. Kimes at MAG 22 (Marine Air Group 22). Kimes was cordial and said he remembered me from flight training at Ewa. He said that he needed dive bomber pilots and that I would be assigned to the Vindicator squadron because I was comparably inexperienced and the most experienced pilots got the better Dauntlesses. He introduced me to Majors Henderson and Norris. Henderson commanded the Dauntlesses and Norris, the Vindicators. Norris briefed me on matters concerning his squadron and said to stand by.

Time goes very slowly when one is waiting under such circumstances; so it was for the best that we were kept busy. The Marine dive bomber air crews worked on the planes, bore-sighted guns, built revetments and fox holes, and sandbagged gun positions. The Marine fighter pilots flew CAP, and the Navy PBY search planes flew patrol from dawn to dusk.

A brief description of the action of June 4, the day of the major attack has already been presented. By nightfall of that day, two-thirds of the Midway Marine air crews and airplanes, including all four squadron leaders, had been lost. The destruction by bombing on Midway Island included demolition of the power house, the seaplane hangers, most of its fuel tanks, utilities, and a large number of other buildings; but its runways went unscathed because the Japanese planned on using them when they captured Midway.

I spent the morning of June 4th during the Japanese attack, sitting in a bomb shelter. In the afternoon after the attack, I helped the fire fighters and worked patching up airplanes returning from battle. That night we were told the wonderful news—the Japanese had lost four aircraft carriers to our Navy and were retreating. One thing we were pretty sure of—the remaining Japanese carrier planes would be destroyed since they now would have no place to land, as previously explained.

With the sinking of the Japanese aircraft carriers on June 4, the battle of Midway was over except for one more American raid the next day, on June 5. The attack was to be made by my group flying what was left of the Midway land-based attack planes which included six Dauntlesses and six shot-up Vindicator dive bombers. Our mission was to sink two heavy cruisers which were running away from the Midway scene as fast as they could. Originally these cruisers, the *Mikuma* and the *Magami*, were scheduled to bombard Midway Island on June 4, but the action was cancelled when the Japanese fleet was ordered to retreat. Both cruisers were big, new, and dangerous. Both had plenty of anti-aircraft protection.

The June 5th action on Midway started at 0300 when all aviation hands were alerted and briefed about the escaping ships. At about 0800 we were told that they would be at a distance of 170 miles on a bearing of 268 degrees from Midway. If WMSB 241 (Marine Bomber Squadron 241, my squadron) took off at 0630 (dawn), it would take a little more than an hour to find them. Captain Marshall Tyler (Major Henderson was dead) was to lead the remaining six Dauntlesses in at 10,000 feet and make orthodox 70-degree dives. Captain Richard Fleming (Norris was also dead) was to follow with the Vindicators and make a gliding attack, because steeper dives might cause the wing fabric to peel off the Vindicators' wings. Since the Japanese had no fighters in the air to harass it, a Dumbo PBY rescue plane was to follow the attack squadron some distance behind to pick up any downed pilots.

At 0630 our twelve planes took off, the Dauntlesses first, followed by the six Vindicators. We climbed to the assigned altitudes. It was a beautiful day. I could see a well-defined horizon in all directions. Only a few fluffy cumulus clouds drifted in the pale blue sky, and the sea looked like a dish of wrinkled blue porcelain. Far ahead of us and high, we could see the Dauntlesses—dark grey specks flying in echelon (a formation in which each plane flies slightly above and to the right of the plane in front). I was flying fourth plane from the front in my group, which was flying the same formation. It was a good formation which permitted the planes to spread out quickly and line up for a dive starting with the front plane, each plane following the other down in order.

The longer we flew and the closer the enemy, the more excited and tense I became; the adrenaline was pumping. I was on a real high with the intense clarity of focused attention, a combat high. The first indication that we had found the enemy was the appearance of tiny black ships on the sea in the distance. They each had curly white wakes behind them like the tails of white horses. The curl was a sign they had spotted us and were taking evasive action. No doubt they had their own search planes in the air. As we drew nearer, the ships became spotted with pin-points of light, like fireflies—their anti-aircraft guns beginning a barrage. Moments later, high and ahead of us the Dauntlesses, which we could see, started their run.

They cascaded straight down, like a shimmering silver waterfall with the sun shining on it. Then, white water spouts geysered all around the ships. Our pilots opened their cockpit canopies. We rolled into a column formation and started letting down on our glide. As we did, the black puffs of exploding anti-aircraft shells appeared around us everywhere. I forgot about everything but the targets, which were enlarging rapidly.

Suddenly I felt a buffeting. We'd been hit, but the controls felt okay. I looked around at the gunner, whose back was turned toward me. The top of his head was gone. When I turned back I saw a stream of smoke coming from the engine, and oil splattered on the windshield. I knew, then, that in only a minute the plane would be in flames. I shut down the engine, turned off the magnetos, closed the gasoline valves, jettisoned the 1,000-pound bomb, unbuckled the seat harness, disconnected the earphones, then stood up—holding onto the top of the windshield, about to jump out. I did this all automatically, without thinking.

Suddenly an anti-aircraft shell blew off the tail of the plane, causing it to flip and make a torque roll to the left, throwing me clear—the best thing that could have happened under the circumstances. It all occurred in seconds. I pulled the rip cord on the parachute immediately because I was so low, and the sea was coming up quickly to meet me.

Then that beautiful chute blossomed out, and I could see my plane nearby, tumbling in flames. I had just enough time to pop the carbon dioxide capsule which blew up my Mae West, a gas-filled life jacket named after the famous full-figured movie actress, before I hit the water. There was a light sea breeze so the chute dragged me a little, which is the luckiest way to land in the water because the parachute doesn't come down on top of one and get all tangled up. I cut the chute loose with my knife and then released the yellow dye marker in the sea. There I was—in the middle of the Pacific!

After what seemed like an hour, Dumbo, the PBY search-and-rescue plane, found me (he had seen my chute). It made a low pass and dropped a life raft into which I scrambled. A few minutes later Dumbo landed near by, and after a little struggle, pulled me inside.

The whole episode was lucky, and I have believed in luck ever since. When people ask me what I thought about, I can't remember thinking anything. It all happened so fast and I reacted so automatically. Two days later I was headed back to Pearl Harbor on a destroyer. I had had a ten-day round trip to Midway—and what a trip!

****

Epilogue: Our squadron inflicted much damage to both ships. Particularly outstanding was our valiant leader and my friend Captain Richard Fleming, who dropped his bomb and got a hit. Immediately after the hit, his plane burst into flames, and he, we thought purposely, dove into the super structure of the Makuma, adding more damage by starting fires all over the ship. All planes got home but three. One other plane was shot down by anti-aircraft fire and the pilot was also rescued by Dumbo.

SIXTEEN

Guadalcanal

In the dive bomber's dream of perfection, the clean blue Dauntlesses—with their perforated dive flaps open at the trailing edges of their wings and their big bombs tucked close and pointing home, the pilot straining forward, rudder-feet and stick-hands light and delicate, getting it just right as the yellow decks come up, left hands that would reach down and forward to release now resting on the cockpit edge, gunners lying on their backs behind the cocked twin barrels searching for the fighters that did not come—carved a moment out of eternity for a man to remember forever.

— Commander Edward P. Stafford, USN,
USS *Enterprise's* Biographer

"Oh, pray for your pal on Guadalcanal..." (U.S. Marine song)

THE GUADALCANAL CAMPAIGN, ACCORDING TO THE great historian Samuel E. Morrison, was the most bitterly contested in American history since the campaign of Northern Virginia during the Civil War. It comprised seven major Naval engagements, at least ten pitched land battles and innumerable forays, bombardments, and skirmishes. It lasted seven months, during which sixty-five major warships were sunk in Iron Bottom Sound, the channel between Guadalcanal and the Florida Islands twenty-five miles to the east. Japanese grand strategy at this time contemplated not only conquering China and neutralizing the United States—in which they were stopped at the battle of Midway—but conquering the entire South Pacific, including Australia and New Zealand. To this end, they had been very successful. For by early summer of 1942, the Japanese had overrun the Philippines, Indonesia, and nearly all of the many Pacific island groups and archipelagoes lying between Japan and Australia, and they were preparing to invade the final gateway islands of New Guinea and Guadalcanal during the month of July, 1942. If this action were successful, Australia would be wide open, with virtually no defenses, since her armies were fighting with the British in North Africa and India.

It was on these two islands, New Guinea and Guadalcanal, that the United States and her allies determined to meet the enemy, hold the line, and reverse the sweeping Japanese invasion. Fighting northward, we would systematically recapture the South Pacific islands in reverse order, leading us to the Japanese homeland. This action was code-named "Watch Tower." The plan was that General MacArthur and his armies would fight their way, starting at New Guinea, recapturing the Philippines, and then possibly proceeding to Okinawa. At the same time, Admiral Nimitz's Navy and Marines would fight their way north (paralleling MacArthur to the east), beginning with Guadalcanal and the rest of the Solomon Islands, then the Gilberts, Marshalls, Carolines, Marianas, Volcano Islands, and finally joining MacArthur and his armies in Okinawa. As it turned out, MacArthur didn't leave the Philippines. However, that's another story.

From Okinawa the United States would attack the islands of Japan. Of course, during this great sweep north, the two invading forces would support each other as necessary, but basically until they joined they were to remain separate operations.

One difficulty in recreating the past is that the reader knows how everything will turn out, so the events have an air of inevitability. This was not true at the time, especially in the case of Guadalcanal. We know now, of course, that Guadalcanal was the pivotal battle of the war. Although it wouldn't have taken place without the triumph at Midway where we stopped the enemy's progress, it was the beginning of our long, hard road to Japan. But victory was very uncertain then. The Japanese seemed invincible, especially in jungle fighting.

Guadalcanal is the center-most island in the 900 mile long Solomon archipelagoes, which consists of a double row of mountainous, volcanic islands running in a southeast direction, beginning just south of the equator and running parallel to, and 1,000 miles from, the northeast coast of Australia. The sea channel running between the two chains of islands became known as the "Slot" because it was a natural funnel for planes and ships attacking southeastward from the great Japanese military base located on Raboul Island in the Bismarck archipelagoes northwest of the Solomons and 600 miles from Guadalcanal. Guadalcanal itself is ninety-two miles long and thirty-three miles wide with a spine of mountains rising to a height of 8,000 feet.

Viewing it from the air or sea, Guadalcanal was a vision of beauty—evil beauty. Once ashore, however, it became something else. Except for occasional patches of shoulder-high kunai grass, the blades of which could cut a person's hand as quickly as a scalpel, the tropical forests swathed the island. From the air it looked solid enough to walk on. In reality, the ground, if you could find it, lay one hundred feet below the cloying beauty of the tree tops—a cathedral of banyans, iplis, and eucalyptus. In between the trees were thick, steamy, matted, almost impenetrable screens of cassia, liana vines, and twisted creepers, masked here and there by mangrove swamps and clumps of bamboo. The green vastness was only broken by streams veining the forests, flowing northward to the sea. The forest was arrogant and malevolent, with a vile stench of rotting undergrowth and stink lilies everywhere.

There were the creatures too: snakes, crocodiles, centipedes, and leeches that crawled across the flesh, leaving a trail of swollen skin. There were scorpions, stinging wasps as long as your finger, spiders as big as your fist, and mosquitoes, mosquitoes, mosquitoes—all carriers of malaria, yellow fever, dengue fever, and filariasis. There were also flies that laid eggs in your food and caused diarrhea, the stool of which could crawl.

The very humid tropical heat was unbearable, and it didn't cool off much at night. In addition, there were all kinds of bacterial and skin infections—finger and toenails would totally disappear. It was twenty years before my nails would grow back without holes in them.

It was into this grotesque setting that 16,000 Marines started landing on August 7, 1942. On July 5, South Pacific reconnaissance planes had gathered a bit of news that sparked off operation Watch Tower: the Japanese were beginning work on an airfield on the north end of Guadalcanal. It would eventually become Henderson Field, named after Major Loften R. Henderson, USMC, the airman killed at Midway. The Japanese expected to have the new Guadalcanal field ready for sixty bombers by August 1 and to have a complete air flotilla based there by the end of the month. That would menace the Allies' entire position in the South Pacific.

The Marines' first mission was to capture the field at the north end of the island and get it into shape for American airplanes to use. They accomplished this task with alacrity. On August 20, the first Marine airplanes arrived. Their arrival was none too soon since the ground Marines had had no air cover since the day they landed and had been attacked daily and almost every night by the Japanese based in the northern Solomons. The Marine air contingent consisted of twelve Dauntlesses and nineteen Wildcat fighters, led by Lt. Col. Richard Mangrum, USMC, who also commanded the Dauntlesses. Captain Bruce Prosser, USMC, was second in command and led the fighters. Fighting the much bigger Japanese air force was a big job for this very small group, but they went into action immediately.

****

After Midway I returned to Hawaii. I had been back about a month when I got new orders: to join a regular scouting squadron on the carrier *Enterprise*, which was somewhere in the South Pacific. I would be a division leader and in command of six of the eighteen Dauntlesses in the squadron. I was exultant. The *Enterprise*! The big E! The biggest, fastest carrier in the fleet. The big time—and a division leader at that. I couldn't believe my luck. This was phenomenal. I would, no doubt, get the latest model Dauntless, which I hadn't seen yet, but was told had a bigger engine than the Dauntless I had flown, had more armor plate, and had twin thirty-caliber machine guns, instead of a single, mounted in the rear seat. Additionally I found out that I was about to be promoted to lieutenant junior grade.

Now I was sorry I'd spent the two weeks on R&R (rest and recreation) lounging around the Royal Hawaiian Hotel sunning, drinking, and girl-chasing instead of spending the month practicing carrier landings and dive bombing the target island of Kaloohawe. Imagine—one's first landing on the *Enterprise* with everybody watching and getting a "wave off" or a "bounder"—showing no class at all because of a bad approach, or missing the second wire with the tail hook and bouncing. Well, I'd practice landing everyday and show a lot of class. After all, I had almost 700 hours and a combat record—not a very glamorous one, I admitted, but it counted. I figured that's probably why I was assigned these great orders.

Two days later I left Pearl Harbor with several other pilots each flying a new Dauntless headed for Noumea, New Caledonia, a free French city about 1,000 miles east of Brisbane, Australia, and a brand new American military staging base. We stopped to refuel at Palmyra Island, south of Hawaii, just below the equator, then on to Samoa, and from there to our destination. Noumea was a medium-size French colonial town and seaport. It was a refuge for the free French (DeGaullists) who had taken over the government and jailed or executed the Petainists, who were puppets of the Germans. It was, from everyone's point of view, strategically located— sort of a guard lying within flying distance of both Australia and Guadalcanal. The U.S. was planning to use Noumea as a huge supply base and the jumping off place for the great sweep north. Almost all U.S. troops, airplanes, and logistical goods landed at Noumea and were then distributed to their destination. It was comfortably tropical like Hawaii and had some good restaurants and beaches.

When we got off the plane at Noumea, we were met by a Navy staff officer who billeted us, gave us each a bottle of whiskey, and told us where to report in the morning. I was tired, so after a good dinner and a few drinks, I went to bed. Some of the others in our party went to town, and the next day had all sorts of wild stories about the French girls, all of which were probably just dreams, if I know naval aviators.

The next day, August 24, 1942, three of us flew our planes to the big E 300 miles north. It was a beautiful day. We took off about 1000 hours and arrived at about noon. When the *Enterprise* saw us coming and CAP cleared us as being friendly, she slowly turned her bow into the wind for our recovery.

I'll never forget the thrill—the big high—my first carrier landing that wasn't a practice and on the big E! We were flying the inverted V formation

An SBD-3 Dauntless dive-bomber of Bombing Squadron 6 prepares for
launch from the carrier USS *Enterprise,* early 1942.

and immediately went into echelon, opening our canopies and spreading out
about two miles apart in the landing circle, flying up the starboard side at
800 feet, coming around the bow, flying downwind on the port side, then
pulling around on base, easing the throttle, dropping the flaps, landing gear,
and hook, and then making the long final approach. The landing signal officer
reminded us to go through the check list again; then signaled to lock in the
glide; and a few seconds later, waving orange paddles horizontally across
his neck signaled to chop the throttle. It was perfect! I caught the second wire
and made the three point controlled crash. In seconds the deck crew
unhooked me and the barrier was raised so I could taxi to a parking spot.
Enterprise was reputed to be a nice ship, having a good ward-room, excellent
food, and ample accommodations. The air crew aboard was supposed to be
made up of five eighteen-plane squadrons: two fighter, one bombing, one
scouting, and one torpedo bombing—a total of ninety planes when all billets
were filled. However, because of the severe losses suffered at Midway,
Enterprise had only about fifty planes when we were welcomed aboard.

I was immediately assigned duty with VS-6. The "6" signified *Enterprise*, and the "VS" indicated scouting squadron. With the addition of us newcomers, VS-6 had about eleven planes instead of the standard eighteen. The squadron leader was Lt. Turner Caldwell, USN. He welcomed us and explained that the small squadron was really made up of eight VS-5 airplanes from *Yorktown* and that we three were the first VS-6 planes. What remained after Midway of the original VS-6 squadron had been sent to Australia for a rest.

Caldwell told us to have some lunch and get some rest because we were going on a late afternoon search-strike mission to look for the Japanese aircraft carrier Ryujo. At about 1600 hours we took off, all eleven of us, each with a 500-pound bomb and a full load of fuel, which gave us a maximum range of about 1400 miles, 700 miles out and 700 miles back. This left about 150 miles reserve to find our aircraft carrier on return. We flew at about 5,000 feet beneath a cloud cover which was beginning to form, holding a tight "V" formation for protection against enemy fighters that might be lurking among the clouds. When in this "V" formation, a group of Dauntlesses with their free-swinging, twin-mounted machine guns supporting each other, could make it very nasty for attacking fighters.

As we flew, the sun went down, the cloud cover lowered, and Caldwell carefully dodged the afternoon tropical thunder storms which were beginning to form. By 1900 hours (7:00 p.m.) the weather was getting dirty. It was beginning to rain, visibility was getting bad, and we had abandoned the V- formation to an echelon, a single line of planes, one behind the other, below and to the right side. In this formation it was much easier to avoid collision in the dark. We'd stopped worrying about enemy fighters, and we couldn't have seen the enemy ship we were looking for if we flew over it. I felt that if we didn't find our target by sundown, we should forget it. But then, I didn't give the orders.

Suddenly the radio came alive with a coded message, followed by a voice message. Caldwell told us by voice that his coded message advised *Enterprise* that due to bad weather, we would not return, but instead would land at the Marine airfield located about fifty miles away on an island called Guadalcanal and requested *Enterprise* to so advise the Marines on the island. Since we were at least 450 miles from the ship, this was good news to us. However, there was always the chance that the radio messages wouldn't get through due to the undependable radio transmission of those days. We couldn't contact the Marines directly because, for some unaccountable reason, Navy airplanes didn't have Marine radio frequencies. If they didn't know we were coming, they would very possibly think we were the attacking enemy—a chilling thought. Caldwell repeated the coded message a few times as we began to get separated. He also told us that the airfield was on the north end of the island and not to fly across the island because it had 8,000 foot high mountains obscured by the clouds.

We were then at about 1,000 feet and dropping. I got out my flashlight and looked over the chart, which wasn't much help since it didn't show Guadalcanal. For the next twenty minutes we were able to keep below the storm clouds and find the southern shore line of the island, which we followed—first to the west and then around to the north. The radio cracked again. This time Caldwell advised that he had sighted the airfield and that we would first drag over it, then spread out in a line in a right hand flight pattern and land.

Immediately after passing the airfield, jeep head lights flashed on, outlining the field. What luck! They must have gotten the message or figured no intelligent enemy would strafe the field at night. Anyway, all eleven Dauntlesses, which became known as Enterprise Flight 300, landed safely in the rain. No question, we were pros, particularly Lt. Turner Caldwell, who later received the distinguished flying cross for his work at Midway and Guadalcanal. He knew his stuff!

The Marines were delighted to see us. The Marine squadron had been on the island four days and consisted of nineteen fighters commanded by Capt. John Smith, USMC, and twelve dive bombers commanded by Major Richard C Mangrum, USMC. Our eleven Dauntlesses doubled their bombing force. Although we planned to return to *Enterprise* the next day, Flight 300 stayed and flew with the Marines until September 27, over a month. I knew just about everybody in both the Marine squadrons. They were at Ewa when I was there, including my very good friend, Major Fletcher Brown, USMC, and a fraternity brother, Charles Kendrick,

USMC. Because of a food shortage, we ate our emergency rations for dinner that first night, drank fermented palm juice—a potent beverage something like strong vodka—and traded stories.

The day we arrived, Smith's Marine fighters had had their first battle with a group of fifteen bombers and twelve fighters from the Japanese carrier we had been looking for, the Ryujo. They were attempting to raid Henderson Field. Smith's fighters downed sixteen enemy planes, but lost some of his own in the process.

The next day I found out under what gross handicaps we were fighting. Henderson Field was either a bowl of black dust that fouled airplane engines or, due to the frequent rain, a quagmire of black mud which made an airplane taking off, particularly when carrying a heavy load, resemble a fly trying to rise from molasses. At that time, there were no bomb hoists, and the 500-pound bomb had to be lugged and loaded by hand. The 1000-pound bombs couldn't be handled at all. The simple act of refueling that small number of planes could take all night since the fuel available was in fifty-five gallon drums from which gas had to be pumped and filtered through a chamois. Radio communications were a nightmare. Navy planes couldn't talk to the field for the reasons already explained. The Marine planes could make scouting reports up to 100 miles out, but could receive signals no more than twenty miles from the field. This meant that a Navy dive bomber on a search-strike mission had to be paired with a Marine plane and, of course, most patrols went a good deal farther than 100 miles. Another problem was that the Navy planes were equipped with a small hard rubber tail wheel needed for carrier landings, and these wheels chewed up the earth runway like plowshares. After a Navy squadron landed, the whole field had to be rolled again.

One thing our fighter pilots had learned from the battles of Coral Sea and Midway was not to dog fight the more maneuverable Japanese Zero fighters single handedly. The ideal tactic was to dive on the enemy bombers, which generally came over in twenty-six plane formations, with a direct overhead or high-side pass to avoid their tail stingers; then dive for home close to your wingman, if possible, and let the Zeros chase you. If a fighter got caught alone by a Zero, and the Zero had a good pilot, he'd get on a Wildcat's tail. Then all the Wildcat could do was dive and call for help. One Zero against one Wildcat wasn't an even fight, but with mutual support, two Wildcats were worth four or five Zeros because they could use the Thatch weave. In this maneuver each plane keeps turning into the other so that an attacker getting on one plane's tail would be immediately exposed to the fixed guns of the defending wing man. Generally this maneuver was used by fighters, but it could be successfully used by dive bombers also.

The slower Dauntlesses were much more vulnerable than the fighter. However, if they gave each other mutual support using the Thatch weave, they could survive. The Zero without self-sealing gas tanks couldn't stand more than one or two seconds of fire from our powerful machine guns which used incendiary bullets; the Zeros would burst into flame. Our Wildcats and Dauntlesses, on the other hand, could handle as much as fifteen minutes of their less powerful gun fire. We had wonderfully rugged planes with self-sealing gas tanks and lots of armor plate around the pilots.

Living conditions on Guadalcanal were appalling. Pilots had to fight and fly all day on a diet of dehydrated potatoes, spam, or cold hash, and sometimes, captured Japanese rice. Most everybody was out of cigarettes (everybody smoked), and frequently the only thing we had were Japanese brands which were awful. Sleep on the mud-floored tents was constantly interrupted by destroyers or submarines that stood off shore and lobbed shells at Henderson Field or by Japanese cruise planes, which we nicknamed "Louie the Louse" and "Washing Machine Charlie," that flew over every night and dropped bombs. There was neither soap nor a safe place to bathe. If one didn't get malaria, he was certain to get dysentery (which I had), and many got both.

For the next two weeks, I flew three patrols a day, carrying a 500-pound high explosive all-purpose bomb. We usually went up the Slot for 300 miles or so looking for troop transports, their destroyer escorts, and submarines. My wing man was 2nd Lt. Jim Wheeler, USMCR, a good looking kid from Princeton, just out of flight school and with about 350 flying hours—very green when compared to my 750 plus hours. Instructions to me were to look after him and train him. My instructions to him were to never take his eyes off me and if attacked by Zeros, to go into the thatch weave, which I had taught him.

On most patrols we wouldn't find many ships; however, on the way home we searched out bodies of enemy troops and strafed them with our fixed guns and dropped our high explosive bombs. Clearly, the reason we didn't encounter many floating targets was because to avoid air attack the Japanese troops and supply ships came south down the Slot at night to unload reinforcements on the west side of Guadalcanal; then they returned north while still under cover of darkness. We controlled the air during the daylight hours; the Japanese navy dominated the Slot at night. In those early days, night fighting techniques and equipment hadn't yet been developed by the United States Navy in the Pacific, although they were being used in Europe.

Twice while on dawn patrol, we caught stragglers scurrying up the Slot towards safety, and we attacked. Neither Jim nor I had the opportunity to do a great deal of damage except I got one shot which severely damaged a loaded troop ship, and I am sure it caused many casualties. Usually on these occasions we didn't return unscathed. One time Jim counted thirty-eight machine gun bullet holes in his wings, and I found not only machine gun holes, but a six inch diameter hole in the port wing made by an anti-aircraft shell which had failed to explode—more luck!

During these weeks two good friends were killed: my first dive bombing instructor, Capt. Fletcher Brown, USMC, who simply disappeared in bad weather while on a search-strike mission and 2nd Lt. John (Red) Kendrick, USMCR, the Stanford fraternity brother who was shot down in a dog fight. He had five victories to his credit, however, before he "bought the farm." ("He bought the farm" was an expression used in World War II to refer to someone who had been killed in battle. It came from the bull sessions during which men asked each other what they were going to do after the war. The usual answer was, "Get married and buy a little farm to live on the rest of my life." "He went west" was the World War I expression. West was the direction of home.)

Although we didn't intercept many ships coming down the Slot, our fighters were kept busy fighting off Japanese bombing raids on Henderson Field. Although we shot down five Japanese planes for every one we lost, the numbers of our planes were diminishing rapidly. During this period the Navy and Marines held on to Guadalcanal by faith rather than reason. One great morale booster was the American Navy's doctrine (as opposed to the Japanese doctrine) that pilots were not expendable—everything possible was done to rescue downed airmen, wherever they were. An example of the great lengths to which Americans would go to save a pilot is an incident that occurred during the time I was stationed at the Canal. About 200 miles up the Slot near the New Georgia Islands, one of a group of Dauntless search planes was nailed by anti-aircraft fire and had to ditch in the channel between the two islands. The plane sank immediately, giving the pilot no time to get his life raft out. So there he was—floating in his Mae West (how well I know the feeling).

The islands on both sides were occupied by thousands of Japanese, many of whom saw him hit the water and with their binoculars could see him bobbing in the waves. His American buddies, including me, saw him go in, and we set up a traffic circle around him for an hour and a half. The wind and the current were carrying the pilot toward one of the islands occupied by the enemy; so a Dauntless dropped him a life raft, and another dropped him a parachute to act as a drogue. During this time, our Dauntlesses shot up any Japanese attempt to get to the downed pilot, including the destruction of a large wooden barge and a couple of rubber boats carrying riflemen. By the time our radio message had reached headquarters, a group of New Zealanders in P40 fighters came over to relieve us. The New Zealanders were wild men. They would weave back and forth, then suddenly attack one of the islands and shoot up the jungle. All this while, the man in the life raft was rowing like mad against the wind.

Finally, the Japanese managed to swing a shore battery around and began peppering the raft, but at the first shot, the New Zealanders went crazy. You'd have thought it was a hundred-million dollar battle ship they were out to protect. They peeled off and dove on that installation until even the trees around the battery fell down. Unfortunately, one P40 fighter burst into flames and augered into the sea.

From then on the New Zealanders were called "the hounds from hell." After an hour, Marine fighters from Guadalcanal relieved the P40s. As they left for home, the New Zealanders buzzed the downed man wagging their wings. The Japanese then opened up with a mortar, and the Marines and their Wildcats went after the mortar like bumble bees. They even made the New Zealanders look conservative. After the mortar was destroyed, they began strafing the beaches up and down, causing pillars of smoke to rise from the unseen targets hidden by the trees. While this was going on a PT boat, with her Packard engines roaring, picked up the downed pilot. All of this for the life of one man.*

The Japanese, on the other hand, did nothing to save their pilots. When one of their planes went down or a pilot bailed out into the ocean, he was through - he never came back. In the Japanese Navy and Army, men were absolutely dispensable. To prove the point, Japanese airplanes were designed with no armor protecting the crew and light metal gas tanks that blew up; whereas, the design of U.S. planes included armor plate around the cockpits and self-sealing, almost explosion-proof fuel tanks.

****

My last flight in the Navy took place September 8, 1942. The weather had been normal for the season. It was bright and clear in the morning, moody and cloudy by early afternoon, followed by thunder storms in the late afternoon, then rain in the evening and all night. The whole cycle started all over again the next day. We'd been having trouble with water collecting in the fifty-five gallon drums in which the airplane fuel was stored. This problem was caused by condensation which was particularly bad in the humid, rainy, steamy weather of Guadalcanal. I always supervised the fueling of my plane to be sure the gasoline was strained through a clean, dry, chamois cloth in order to keep the water from going into the tank with the gasoline. I felt I had to be particularly observant because we were running out of chamois cloth.

When I went out to my airplane at about 1600 hours to get ready for evening patrol, the mechanic, who had been pre-flighting my plane, advised me that he'd found a crack in its exhaust manifold and that it would take at least two hours to fix, provided he could salvage another manifold. He

---

* The rescued man, himself told me the story of what happened after I left the scene with the Dauntlesses. He also was interviewed by James Michener, the famous author who published the story with some embellishment in novel form.

told me that I'd have to take another plane, which I certainly didn't want to do, but had no choice since operations had assigned me a beaten-up Marine Dauntless that had been standing out in the weather. When I talked to the mechanic who took care of it, he said it was fueled and ready to go. We pre-flighted it together, drained the water out of the tanks, or at least tried to, and I started the engine. Everything seemed fine, but I was really angry about the plane having been fueled recently, which meant any water in the fuel might not have settled out completely.

I took off at about 1630 hours with my wingman, Jim. I didn't have an observer with me, but he did. We headed for the Slot. We flew west around Cape Esperance, south to Cape Hunter, and saw nothing. Then, in the rain we headed up the Slot at an altitude of about 1500 feet with a 2000-foot ceiling. The plane wasn't in very good shape. The tachometer didn't work; the shoulder harness was defective, you couldn't lean forward in it very well; the electric bomb release was inoperative; plus a few minor problems such as broken fuel gauges. But worst of all, the radio receiver kept cutting out.

After an hour and a half, when we were opposite the New Georgia Islands, I decided we couldn't see anything, so we might as well go home. The weather was much more dangerous than the Japanese. Reportedly, but not advertised, was the fact that only two out of ten pilots were killed in combat. The rest died from flying in bad weather, getting lost and running out of fuel, or blowing a landing, particularly on a carrier.

On the return trip we were flying at about a 1,000 feet over the water with approximately a mile visibility—not too bad; but it would be dark when we got back to the field at 1930 hours. We were about half-way home when the engine sputtered. For a moment I thought it was over. I maneuvered the throttle and mixture lever and the engine roared back to normal; but then it sputtered a little more. Water in the fuel! I was sure of it. "Why in hell did I ever take this plane?" I asked myself. "I knew better! This is the worst that could happen—down in the Slot all night with little chance of being picked up. This might have been what happened to Fletcher Brown." Fortunately at this moment, my radio transmitter was working. I radioed Jim and asked him to call the base and tell them I might be landing on the field in the wrong direction or might not get back at all. He wagged his wings that he

Aftermath of air raid on Guadalcanal.

understood. My heart was beating hard. My hands became clammy in their gloves. The adrenaline was running fast. I was furious with myself; I knew you couldn't trust anybody in this business. I'd been trained to know it.

We passed the Russell Islands and I began to feel better—closer to home. We were down to about 500 feet altitude when we finally came to Cape Esperance, the northern tip of Guadalcanal. The engine was sputtering intermittently, but was holding on. I just needed twenty-five miles more. The sun was down, not that we ever saw it on this trip. It was dark, and we were directly over Japanese-held beaches. If I ditched around here I'd be captured—if I didn't drown. In any event, it was pretty hard to ditch at night.

Ten minutes more…five minutes more…three minutes more…and the damned engine quit!

I could see car headlights ahead, outlining the threshold of the field through the darkness. Earlier I had jettisoned my bomb to lighten the plane.

I now opened the canopy and fired a red parachute flare in the air with my Very gun. *Maybe someone will see it*, I thought. I knew I couldn't make the field since this plane glided like a brick, but I would get as close as I could. I put the plane in the flattest glide possible and kept the flaps and wheels up. There was also the hope the engine might still catch; so I didn't turn off the fuel, mag, or throttle.

Then I began clipping the tree tops, and I knew the jig was up. I wasn't more than a quarter of a mile from the headlights. At least I was in home territory. I turned off the fuel, mag, and cut the throttle so the plane wouldn't catch fire. The next instant, I was plowing into the jungle. The plane lost a wing, spun around and landed nose down about ten feet off the ground, hanging in the vines which had somewhat cushioned what would otherwise be a very violent landing. The lights went out for me because the shoulder restraining harness broke and I hit my head against the cowling.

The next thing I knew, I heard voices—speaking English. It was a Marine rescue party that had just arrived. They'd gotten Jim's message, had seen the flare, ran up the beach, and cut their way through the jungle to the plane. I don't know how they ever found it at night, even though it wasn't very far in from the beach. That beautiful lady luck was riding in the Dauntless with me—again.

The plane, of course, was totaled, but I only suffered a bloody face, the loss of two front teeth, sprained wrists, and a terrible headache. I wasn't able to climb out of the cockpit because of my wrists and dizziness, but the boys had no trouble getting me out and back to the hospital tent. The next morning I had a seizure—it resembled an epileptic fit. The doctor said it wasn't epilepsy, but was caused by brain damage of some kind and, my flying days were over. To make things worse, I began showing symptoms of malaria, which apparently had been suppressed up to that time by taking a daily dose of quinine. Fortunately, the malaria turned out to be a mild case; however, for the rest of the war and about ten years thereafter, I had three or four malaria attacks a year, each of which sent me to bed for two or three days. On September 10th, I was fortunate to be flown to New Caledonia, where I joined a contingent of casualties being sent to Pearl Harbor

SEVENTEEN

Oak Knoll Hospital, Oakland, California

I N MID-SEPTEMBER I WAS ADMITTED TO THE NAVAL HOSPITAL at Pearl Harbor for observation and treatment, which consisted of bed rest with ice packs on my head. The hospital was overflowing with casualties from Guadalcanal, but somehow I rated a bed instead of a cot in a hall or on a porch. Needless to say, I was lonesome and depressed because I kept having seizures, and it didn't seem that I had much of a future. In fact, none of the M.Ds thought I did either. Concussion patients usually ended up in the Veterans Administration hospitals for life. They were generally called shell-shock victims. The one exception to my gloomy prognosis came from Barney Silver, who said I could be cured. He greatly aided my sinking morale.

Barney Silver was a very personable and competent naval reserve physician who had been assigned my case. Barney had practiced medicine in Los Angeles prior to joining the Navy. He was an urologist but was a fine general practitioner too. He had numerous contacts in the medical world, and these included some members on the staff of Oak Knoll, a brand new naval hospital located in Oakland, California. Oak Knoll had a group of specialists for injuries such as mine. In fact, Barney's younger brother,

Sydney, was on that staff as a psychiatrist. Barney wrote him about me and Sydney answered, advising that a famous brain surgeon from a clinic in Kansas City was to be head of the surgical team at Oak Knoll. Accordingly, Barney arranged for me to be transferred from Pearl Harbor to Oak Knoll instead of the old naval hospital in San Diego. When he said good-bye, Barney gave me instructions to take his brother Sid out and get him "bred."

There was one more bright light in my life at the time and that was a correspondence I'd been keeping up with a girl living in the San Francisco Bay Area. Her name was Jean Birkland. I'd received a Christmas card from her in December of 1941, and we'd been corresponding ever since. Her letters always brightened my day and were of particular help now.

I'd met Jean a number of years before, 1931 I believe, when I visited my Grandfather and Grandmother McCandless during the summers when he was working as a project manager on state highway construction jobs in rural California areas. During the summers, Jean often visited her father, who was a state resident engineer. For several years her father and my grandfather worked on the same projects; therefore, for two or three summers in our junior high school years, Jean and I were together a week or two during summer vacation. We spent our time swimming, visiting, and going on picnics together.

She was a dazzling blonde, a year ahead of me in school, and the kind of girl that had a date every night with older boys. I didn't figure I had much of a chance with her, so I didn't really try. We were, however, good friends. Once, I visited her in Berkeley at her home; and once when she visited some friends in Los Angeles, we had a date and went dancing. We lost track of each other in about 1934 when she and her family moved to Baton Rouge, Louisiana. She spent the rest of her school years in Louisiana, and got her degree in art from Louisiana State University. She then moved back to California and became a school teacher about the time I went to Hawaii and joined the Navy.

Our friendship was renewed in 1941, after Pearl Harbor. My Grandmother McCandless, who had kept up correspondence with Jean's family, asked Jean to write to me; thus the Christmas card. I answered her, and we started a rather brisk correspondence which was carried on all through 1942.

Because censorship forbade me revealing my activities or whereabouts, she didn't know my location or what I was doing.

It was the middle of November when I got orders to Oak Knoll Hospital, and by this time I was up and walking around. The transportation I was afforded was aboard the USS *Henderson*, a rather small, pleasant, passenger steamer regularly used for transporting service men's dependents. I was treated as an ambulatory patient passenger with instructions to report to the ship's doctor, who gave me medication daily. Before I left Honolulu, I sent Jean, who was then living in Berkeley, a cablegram advising her of my arrival date as a patient in the naval hospital in Oakland. The trip was uneventful. All I remember about it was reading my first Hemingway book, *Death in the Afternoon*, and that we had a good Thanksgiving Day dinner on board. I arrived on time in Oakland, November 28, 1942.

Oak Knoll was a brand new hospital, and I was the second officer patient admitted to the psychiatric wing. The other officer, a Lt. Commander Baldo, USN, was also a concussion patient. He was a submarine captain who had been in a badly depth-bombed sub in the western Pacific and had the same symptoms I had. Actually, he was worse off than I because he couldn't get out of bed. Because the hospital was fully staffed with young nurses who had no one else to look after, we were smothered with attention and care. I was surprised to discover I had known one of the nurses in high school. The evening of the day I arrived, Jean phoned me and said she had some friends who were willing to drive her out to see me that night. I was all for that.

She arrived about an hour later—vivacious and beautiful! She brought flowers, and we talked while I ate dinner in my room. I remember giving her my chocolate mousse dessert. (I'm still feeding her chocolate.) She told me about her roommate, Helen Lescisin, the rooming house they lived in near Sather Gate on the U.C. Berkeley campus, and her teaching job at Richmond High School in Richmond, a community on the San Francisco Bay about ten miles north of Berkeley.

From then on, Jean came to see me every night and on weekends. She didn't have a car so she came the twenty miles from her school to the hospital via bus and street car. With all the stops those vehicles made, it must have taken her three and a half to four hours to get to the hospital and probably two hours to get home.

The nurses seemed a little touchy about Jean's coming every day, especially if they came into my room while I was kissing her. I guess they felt it was *their* territory. Men were still scarce; even men who were out of action were interesting to them. However, with the Guadalcanal battle going on, that was soon to change.

Barney's brother, Sydney Silver, arranged to be my psychiatrist, and he and Jean soon became friends. Sydney was a very pleasant, cordial, kind and scholarly young man about twenty-five, and we became friends immediately. His only other patient at the time was Lt. Commander Baldo; so he spent a lot of time talking to me.

One night Jean showed up with her roommate Helen, whom she introduced to Sid. Helen and Sid hit it off right away, and from then on Helen frequently came to the hospital with Jean.

The day after I was admitted to the hospital, I was visited by Lt. Commander Durant, Medical Corps., USN, who was to be my top consultant and surgeon, if I needed one. He looked to be between thirty-five and forty and was very friendly and professional. He'd been practicing brain surgery in Kansas City with his brother and father in their own clinic. He scheduled me for a series of physical examinations and tests and explained that some of them would be painful and make me very sick. (This was before the day of the electroencephalogram.) One of these exams required draining out all of my spinal fluid and replacing it with dye for brain x-rays—the most painful thing I've ever endured. The exam did indeed make me very ill and nauseous for several days. My misery wasn't in vain, however, because it was that test that revealed the problem! Dr. Durant said that he had discovered a subdural hematoma over my left ear which he believed he could successfully remove. The clot had pushed my brain against my skull on the right side of my head.

On December 15,1942, Dr. Durant operated on me by drilling a three-quater inch hole in my skull, which enabled him to remove a large blood clot and other extraneous material. Baldo underwent this same operation. Apparently the operation posed some dangers because the hospital asked Jean to notify my grandparents and suggested they be present during the surgery, which they all were—Grandfather and Bidy McCandless and Grandfather Sprague. Within a few days I had recuperated from the operation enough to be ambulatory. The headaches and seizures stopped, and by New Years Day I was able to visit Jean in Berkeley. I was thin and had a shaved head, but felt fine.

Soon Jean and I were double-dating with Helen and Sydney. We went dancing at the Mark Hopkins, dined at Trader Vic's, and listened to Lou Waters Jazz at the Dawn Club in San Francisco. Jean and Helen particularly liked the Iron Pot Cafe; however, since it was off-limits to naval personnel, we couldn't go there.

During the first week of February following the operation, I was checked out to see if I was psychologically all right. I took a whole battery of tests, including I.Q. and dexterity tests, all of which came out fine. It was the first time I knew my I.Q., but I've forgotten it now.

On February 22, I came before a medical board which explained that although my tests came out well, I could have a medical discharge with disability pay for the rest of my life. Such a discharge was not acceptable to me. I wished to go back to active duty, so I turned down the offer. They said that in any event I could do no more flying and had to stay out of submarines. I said I would appreciate their help in getting my engineer commission restored so I could become a Seabee. The board kindly agreed to all my requests in exchange for a promise that I'd report any further problems to a Navy doctor.

On March 8, 1943, my commission was changed to Lieutenant (jg) Civil Engineer Corps., USNR, and I was released from the hospital with orders to report to the 89th Construction Battalion (Rehabilitation), Camp Parks, California, which was located near Pleasanton in the Bay Area, halfway between Dublin and Livermore and about ten miles east of San Leandro.

****

Helen and Sid were married in November 1943. Lieutenant Commander Baldo survived his operation and was assigned to a non sea-going submarine staff.

Camp Parks, CA, circa 1942. Administration buildings under construction.
(Courtesy of the U.S. Navy Seabee Museum, Port Hueneme, CA)

EIGHTEEN

Camp Parks, California

CAMP PARKS WAS THE WEST COAST BASE FOR THE United States Naval Construction Battalions. Here new recruits were trained, new battalions formed, and existing battalions reformed. It was a large base with the capacity to accommodate twenty battalions (20,000 men) at one time. It was also an R&R station for men returning to the U.S. after twelve to eighteen months of overseas duty in hardship locations, as well as the permanent base for the 89th Seabees, the special Rehabilitation Battalion to which I was assigned until I got my strength back.

Camp Parks was ideally located to provide good access to airports and railroads for those going home on leave and convenient daily transportation to the many forms of recreation in the area. At the same time, it was out in the country with plenty of space for a large base to comfortably carry on military training without disturbing or endangering civilians.

A Construction Battalion consisted of 1,100 to 1,200 men organized into five companies of about 220 men each: Headquarters Company and four construction companies A through D. It must have been the finest military engineering organization in the world. Every recruit was an expert craftsman—even the laborers were trained in construction. The officers were all civil engineers or experienced contractors, and the men came from every building trade: heavy equipment operators, plumbers, cabinet makers, deep-sea divers, blacksmiths, machinists, steel workers, explosive experts, surveyors, etc. The personnel in each battalion was balanced so it was self-sufficient and could undertake any type of project assigned. The battalions were excellently furnished with the best tools and equipment available— complete with spare parts. However, if a spare part wasn't available, a Seabee machinist could probably make it.

The mission of Construction Battalions was to follow the Marines into an island they had captured and, as soon as the area was cleared of enemy troops, start building the necessary facilities to accommodate a military base. Seabees were not supposed to fight; they were too valuable for that. They were, however, armed and trained to defend themselves if trapped by the enemy and hold on until help arrived. A battalion was provided with and taught to use carbines, hand-guns, light machine guns, and mortars. Seabees then underwent the typical military basic training such as marching and parading, and they were conditioned to march ten miles with a full pack. The average age of a Seabee was twenty-six, compared to a Marine or a sailor whose average age was twenty-one.

The name Seabees, by which the organization was best known, is an acronym for Construction Battalion (C B). Each Battalion had a flag emblazoned with its own individual logo and motto. The logos usually displayed, in some form, a bumble bee carrying a machine gun and wearing a sailor's hat.

Since I was a civil engineer, I was very pleased to be in a construction outfit like this. I felt I really belonged, and I'd be getting training I could use after the war. I thought it would be almost as exciting as flying but not as dangerous, and it was probably just as well for me not to stretch my luck any further. I'd had too many close calls. Almost all the people I'd trained with at Ewa were dead now, including the instructors. Those were tough days for Navy airmen.

I reported to the 89th Construction Battalion (Bat Out of Hell) and was told I'd be on leave for a couple of weeks, then I would join the advanced training detachment. During most of my leave I hung around Jean's apartment while she and Helen worked. Generally I shopped and cooked dinner for the three of us, but once in a while we went out to eat. If I was coming from the base I usually brought some steaks since I was on good terms with the Battalion cook. This pleased the girls immensely because meat was hard for them to get under the wartime rationing. During this time, Jean and I discussed marriage, but I demurred because I wanted to be sure I could be restored to good health. If the seizures returned, I figured I was a cooked goose.

Before I returned to duty I visited my mother and my grandparents. Mother was glad to see me, but pretty sick, and she appeared to be deteriorating. This grieved me deeply.

I returned to duty the last week of March and joined the advanced training group. The course covered weaponry, a review of naval regulations, court-martial proceedings, and practice in marching in a variety of ceremonial parade formations. We completed the three-week course in mid-April, 1943, at which time I was assigned permanent duty as officer in charge of station construction equipment and the motor pool. This job included overseeing all the shops as well as the fuel supplies, the latter of which entailed the difficult task of administering the gasoline rationing program.

I had custody of the gasoline rationing coupons, each good for five gallons. The coupons were to be passed out only to people stationed at Camp Parks who had private vehicles and lived off the base with their families. They were entitled to only enough gas to enable them to get to their home and back on liberty days. All others leaving the base on liberty were to use the station liberty bus that made a round-trip between the base, San Francisco, and Oakland every few hours. As can be imagined, the gas coupons were in tremendous demand, not only by potential users but by both military and civilian black marketeers. I had to resist all sorts of pressure: money, food, girls, gifts of all kinds, and various other petty bribes; and I did. I kept the coupons in a safe, the combination to which only one other person had—my office manager, Storekeeper 1st Class John Cruise. I had to trust somebody, but even then I only left the number of coupons I thought he would need while I was gone. The rest I hid.

It was my first experience with the black market. I'd never even heard of such a thing, and I was naive enough to find it hard to believe Americans would carry on such a trade during a war—more culture shock. I was getting tougher and more cynical all the time.

The next sixteen months (April 1943 to August 1944) were very busy and full of fun. I can't say it was carefree because we all knew I'd go overseas again after a year. In fact, I wanted front line battalion experience before the war was over. In April my health was the best it had been since before Pearl Harbor. My headaches were gone; I regained my normal weight; every week I was marching ten miles with a sixty-pound pack; and, best of all, I no longer had signs of the seizures.

About the first of May, I suggested to Jean that we get married the following weekend. She said no because she had a hair appointment that weekend and proposed that we get married the following weekend. That was a duty weekend for me, but I decided to get a friend to stand in for me. Neither of us had time to get our marriage license during the week, so we decided to meet on the Saturday morning of May 15, 1943, on the Oakland Court House steps in plenty of time to get the permit before the license window closed at noon. I, of course, was there promptly on time. Jean was not. I waited and smoked and waited and smoked. I don't know how long I waited, but when Jean finally arrived at about five minutes before noon, she commented that the courthouse steps looked like snow with all my cigarette butts. I still hadn't gotten used to her habit of always being late, but I was so relieved to see her that I couldn't get angry.

That afternoon we surprised Helen while she was talking to an Avon lady who was selling cosmetics. We told Helen that we wanted her to come with us right away because we were going to get married. The Avon lady gave Jean her first wedding gift, a small lipstick sample, then quickly packed her paraphernalia and left. Then the three of us walked to the rectory of a little church nearby where the preacher, Dr. Stanley Hunter, performed the ceremony with his wife and Helen acting as witnesses. That evening Helen, Sid, Jean, and I went to Trader Vic's in Oakland for our wedding dinner, to the Mark Hopkins Hotel in San Francisco for dancing, and then back to Berkeley.

All this time Jean and Helen had lived in the fourth story attic of an old house which was owned by a Mrs. Petger, a very eccentric woman. It had been converted to, or more accurately was being used as, a rooming house. The place was so run down that we called it "Petger Palace." Fortunately, a first-floor room, which was originally the dining room, had been recently vacated; so Jean and I rented it.

We bought some paint: one can of white, one can of watermelon red, and one can of turquoise blue. We painted the ceiling and top part of the plaster walls white, the six -foot wainscoting red, and the floor turquoise blue. It was wild—and boy was Petger mad! We set up housekeeping with a gas cooking stove, a table, a bed, and a couple of chairs. We even had access to a community bathroom—what more could we want? We were delighted. Jean kept her job, and I got home every other night and alternate weekends.

The next thing we acquired was a dog—a Chihuahua. We obtained him in Mountain View one evening when I took Jean down the peninsula for dinner at L'Omelette, my favorite restaurant in college days. We named him Pancho. He was always shivering and was afraid of everybody. At night he slept under the covers at the foot of our bed; in the daytime, on the bed; and when we had company, under the bed.

About this time, I was promoted from lieutenant junior grade to full lieutenant, which is the naval rank equivalent to an Army or Marine captain. In a Battalion, a lieutenant was company commander and was given his own projects to build. He had full responsibility for the design and construction of major structures and had little or no supervision.

One of my station duties was to serve on the naval base Inquest Board, which investigated the deaths of men on the station. With 20,000 people on board, there were bound to be some casualties. Of course we weren't concerned with deaths by natural causes; these, the medical officers took care of. Our concern was deaths by accident and suicide, and we were especially on the look-out for murder. We generally had about one suicide a month, and they usually occurred just before a Seabee unit embarked for overseas duty. Whenever possible, we interviewed the deceased man's friends and usually found that he was single, a brooder, and terribly afraid of being shipped out. Death was usually caused by hanging and took place in some out-of-the-way location like a boiler room or closet. Occasionally, a man would slash his wrist after he'd been drinking heavily. The inquest party had to view the scene, attend the autopsy, and write a report. Almost all the deaths were determined to be suicide; however, we did investigate a few murders which resulted from violence, including shooting and knife fighting.

For the fourteen months we were stationed at Camp Parks, Jean and I enjoyed a very active social life. The officer's club had bang-up dinner parties each month. Everybody dressed up, ate, drank, and danced until 0100. We had our own crowd of married Navy people like ourselves. When there wasn't a station party, we often entertained our friends at Petger Palace, much to Mrs. Petger's distress.

We also had another entirely separate social crowd—Jean's friends who had lived around Berkeley. Some of them were in the Army, but most were civilians. Many had gone to Berkeley High and some had gone on U.C. Berkeley. I was the only Stanford person present, so I generally took a beating. They gave excellent parties, and we were often included. Our principal friends in the group were Betty and Mel Jones, both childhood friends of Jean's. Betty's brother, Walt, married Jean's sister, Marion.

Sometime early in 1944, we bought a used car. Because of the public's difficulty in obtaining gas, second-hand cars were cheap and easy to get. The car was a beauty—a green four-door Buick convertible sedan. It was a 1936 model with a straight eight engine and was as big as a Packard. I took it to the mechanics at the Camp Parks shops, and the boys put it in first-class shape.

Shortly thereafter I got leave, and we went to Los Angeles for a week to visit my mother and Grandparents Sprague. Our wedding had been without the customary ceremony—no family or frills—which was the way we wanted it. We didn't notify anyone of our wedding plans and afterward sent them all telegrams announcing our marriage. I believe Grandmother and Grandfather Sprague were a little disappointed, not because I married Jean, but because I got married at all. They never said as much, but I always felt they expected me to stay at home and take care of them and my mother in their old age. They were, however, pleasant and treated Jean cordially.

While there, we went dancing at the Hollywood Palladium with my

The author and his new bride, the former Jean Birkland, 1944.

cousins, Nancy and Charlotte Brown, and their dates who were second lieutenants in the Army Tank Corps. Later we were told they both had been killed on Omaha Beach during the Normandy invasion.

When we got back to Camp Parks, I was decorated twice at a formal parade: first with the Purple Heart and then the Bronze Star. A few days later I received orders to the 51st Naval Construction Battalion. All good things come to an end, but this transfer was at my request. Jean cried and I was sad; but it was 1944 and I really felt I had to move out to the action.

The 51st had been in the Aleutians for a year and a half and had returned to Camp Parks for rejuvenation and refitting. They were basically a first-class airfield construction outfit—very well disciplined and snappy. I was third from the top in rank, but the youngest lieutenant (twenty-six) and was assigned as Company A Commander. This caused some resentment among

Capt. J. D. Wilson presents the Purple Heart to Lieut. Charles McCandless, of Berkeley, who was wounded in the December 7 attack on Pearl Harbor.—Tribune photos by Bill Crouch.

Newspaper clipping of the author receiving his Purple Heart for wounds received during the attack on Pearl Harbor.

the other company commanders, but in the Navy, rank means rank. I reported only to the Commanding Officer, Commander G. Wood Smith, USNR, and his Executive Officer, Lt. William Montgomery, USNR. Both gentlemen were in their early forties. Two weeks after I joined, we got orders to report to our port of embarkation—Port Hueneme, South of Oxnard, California.

NINETEEN

Camp Hueneme

THE BEGINNING OF JUNE, JEAN AND I SAID GOOD-BYE TO all our friends and Petger Palace, packed the car with our belongings, including Pancho, and headed for Southern California. It was about a seven hour trip to Oxnard, where we stayed in a resort near the beach.

We, not unexpectedly, discovered no pets were allowed. We took care of this by having Jean put Pancho in a zippered satchel and rush upstairs with it while I distracted the desk clerk. We took him out for his evening walk the same way which worked fine at first. Then we felt we had to change our tactics. We hung a fishing line out the window and hauled the satchel up and down, which worked fairly well except that Pancho constantly sabotaged us by unzipping the satchel and sticking his little head out. Eventually, however, we were caught by the maid who unexpectedly walked in on us. From then on, I kept Pancho in my tent at the base and had my steward look after him.

Port Hueneme was a major port of embarkation for Seabees headed for combat duty in the Pacific. It was a camp made up of house tents neatly lined up in rows and columns. The camp accommodated six battalions, each with its own headquarters and mess facilities. The battalions were arranged around a large parade ground, and the camp headquarters buildings were located on the edge of the grounds.

On the waterfront behind the battalions there were huge warehouses and an enormous stock of power equipment: hundreds of bulldozers, diesel shovels, dump trucks, graders, jeeps, and all the tools and spare parts needed for construction. As each battalion got its embarkation date, it assembled its equipment and combat loaded (loading in reverse sequence of the way one wants to unload) its own victory ship, which was a freighter designed for this particular job. Each ship carried one completely equipped battalion. While we were waiting for the day of embarkation, the daily routine for the enlisted men was two hours marching and rifle practice in the morning; then at noon 50% of the crew went ashore until 0630 the next morning. The remaining 50% did the housekeeping, stood perimeter guard, and relaxed. The officers had the same hours; however, they spent it planning the combat loading, selecting equipment, making lists of spare parts they thought they'd need, and doing the usual endless Navy paper work.

The 51st Battalion was in Hueneme about two and a half months. For the first month Jean stayed in the Oxnard Hotel. As departure time edged up (we didn't know the date), we realized she would have to get settled, and she didn't want to stay in Oxnard. Jean chose the Beverly Hills area to live and rented a room with boarding arrangements in a very nice private home which belonged to a lady named Betty Hawkins. I had five days off, so we packed up again and moved her there.

Next she got a job working for a famous interior designer, Paul Frankl, who had a beautiful shop on Rodeo Drive in Beverly Hills, catering principally to the movie star trade, which I felt was a good setup for Jean to spend the duration. I was able to get home to see her every other night and usually got off on the weekends; so we had a lot of time together. Jean always told me about the movie stars who came into the shop. One Saturday, Paul Frankl invited us to cocktails and dinner at Romanoff's Restaurant with one of his famous movie star clients, Charles Laughton. We had a most enjoyable time and Mr. Laughton was very charming. In those days, Romanoff's and the Brown Derby were well-known restaurants that Hollywood celebrities frequented.

Back on the base I kept very busy getting my Company A ready to go overseas. One day after parade a sailor from C Company approached me, saluted, and asked if he could talk to me about a friend who was in the brig (Navy jail), Benny Goldfarb, Carpenter's Mate, 3rd Class from C Company. Benny was going to be court-martialed and needed an officer to act in his defense. He wanted to know if I would do this for him. I was surprised and pointed out that I was an engineer, not a lawyer, and had no experience in this sort of thing. He explained that Benny didn't like officers (probably because he was afraid of them) but that he had been told that he had to have an officer defend him. Benny had heard that McCandless was more interested in the welfare of enlisted men than some of the others and that it was likely that he would represent him fairly.

"Please help Benny, Mr. McCandless, he's in a hell of a lot of trouble," he said.

"Well, let's sit down somewhere and you tell me all about it," I replied. "What's the charge?"

"Attacking a chief petty officer from C company and hitting him over the head with a bottle. I suppose it's attempted murder."

"What's the story?"

He told me what happened: "Benny was asleep in his bunk last Saturday night when the chief came into his tent about 1:00 a.m., crazy drunk. He threw Benny out of his bed and told him he'd just screwed his wife and that she was pretty good for a god-damned Jew. Benny got furious! He grabbed a full quart bottle by the neck and slammed the chief over the head. It cut him up and knocked him out."

"Were there any witnesses?" I asked.

"Petty Officer Jones was asleep in the same tent, and he woke up to see Benny standing over the chief, kicking him. There's apparently no question that Benny did it," he explained.

"Do you believe Benny's story?" I asked.

"Sure! The chief has had it in for Benny for a long time," he quickly replied.

"Why?"

"I don't know, but the chief's known throughout the battalion as being sort of a bastard," he said.

"How's the chief now?"

"He's okay—just some cuts in the scalp."

"Let's go see Benny," I said.

"Then you'll take the case?"

"I'd like to talk to Benny first."

We went over to the camp brig where I found Benny alone in a cage looking down and out. Much to my surprise, he was a small man, had a mild personality, spoke with a strong Brooklyn accent, and trembled as he told me his story, which agreed with the story I had already heard. Benny handed me a copy of the charges submitted to the court-martial board by our Commanding Officer, G. Wood Smith, which suggested attempted murder and assaulting a superior officer and recommended a full court-martial. After I thought about it awhile, I told Benny I'd take the case.

In these days, there were three courts of justice for enlisted men in the Navy. The lowest was a Captain's Mast, which handled misdemeanors such as a day's absence without leave or talking back to an officer. The commanding officer, or executive officer of the Battalion, questioned the accused and accuser and meted out appropriate punishment The maximum punishment for Captain's Mast was a month or two in the brig or a fine of a few months' pay. The second level of justice was a Summary Court-Martial, also handled within the Battalion itself. It had a prosecutor, defense advisor, and a court of five commissioned officers from the Battalion. It had jurisdiction over crimes from a misdemeanor to a felony, and it meted out penalties of as much as a year in the local brig, six months fine, or restriction to base. The Full Court-Martial was principally for felonies and was handled by professional Navy lawyers. It could award a penalty of life in a federal penitentiary or, in some cases, even death.

The next day I went to camp headquarters and talked the case over with a professional court-martial prosecutor. He read the charges and listened to my account of Benny's story. He said he would talk to the participants and the only witness, then decide what the charges should be. Off hand, he believed that the appropriate charge was aggravated assault, which should be tried by a Summary Court instead of a Full Court.

Sure enough, that's what the charge was. I got full credit from Benny's friends for getting the case into the lower court and full discredit from Commander Smith.

"McCandless, goddamn it! " Smith said to me. "I wanted that man court-martialed for trying to commit murder—and upon a superior—that's not the worst of it! How in hell can we keep discipline? In taking this case, you're opposing me—your commanding officer!"

"Sir, I really didn't have any intention of that. I'm simply defending a man who requested I do it, in accordance with Navy regulations," I explained.

"Now you're pulling the book on me, Mac, and I won't have that either," he fumed.

Winning that case was duck soup. Even the prosecutor was on my side when I got through interrogating "poor little Benny" and asking each man on the jury what he would have done if he'd been the defendant.

Commander G. Wood Smith never forgave me. "Every man who gets in trouble is going to come to you! I won't have it! I want real justice done. The men should be punished! McCandless, as of now, you're the Battalion Prosecutor." And, so it was.

Our executive officer, William Montgomery, known as Monty, was a short, heavy set, balding man in his early forties but who looked fifty. He was a civil engineer from New Orleans, had spent his civilian career working for the Atlantic Gulf and Pacific Dredging Company, and was, therefore, highly experienced in waterfront work. I replaced him as Company A commander after he was promoted to Battalion executive officer, while he was still only a lieutenant (it was a lieutenant commander's job). Monty was a pretty heavy drinker and kept a bottle of whiskey in his desk drawer. He'd never been married, and in the evenings before dinner he'd sit at a table in the officer's club by his half empty bottle of whiskey and eye the wives of the junior officers. Then he'd shake his head and tell his tale of loneliness and woe to anybody who would listen. He liked me and I liked him, so I often sat down with him. He always told me what a lucky dog I was to have such a beautiful wife and would some day have children. In fact, if he were drunk enough, he'd almost cry. As an executive officer, he was mild and fair, and he helped moderate many of the wild ideas and fits of bad temper coming from the commanding officer. I always got along well with Monty.

At Camp Hueneme our house tent billets were maintained by black stewards. As a commander, I had my own steward who shined by shoes, took care of my clothes and laundry, made my bed, cleaned the tent, and polished my guns. During meals, he waited on table at the officer's club.

One morning after parade when Pancho the Chihuahua was living with me, I had to leave camp for a while. I left Pancho in my tent, tethered to the leg of my bed. For some reason while I was away, my steward lifted the bed leg; the leash came off the leg; and Pancho ran out the door and out into tent city. He scared the daylights out of the steward, who hadn't noticed the dog under the bed.

The steward took off for headquarters where he found Monty enjoying his bottle. Monty, apparently three sheets to the wind, called out the guard, the camp fire department, and the officer of the day. He then commandeered some jeeps, and the big hunt through the entire camp began. They never did find Pancho that day, but I found him the next day in the custody of a sailor in another battalion. It was a good thing I found him because I was otherwise in a fix with Jean. I didn't dare return to her without the dog.

Monty's wild search resulted in not only disturbing the whole camp, but smashing up two jeeps, which collided head-on coming around a blind corner. The camp commanding officer was an admiral who then jumped all over the 51st Battalion, infuriating Commander Smith. He called me in and told me to get "that damned dog" out of camp. Fortunately, Jean had just moved to Beverly Hills, so I took Pancho there.

TWENTY

Sailing to Ulithi

THE MIDDLE OF AUGUST WE GOT WORD WE'D BE LEAVING SOON. Security was tightened. No leaves longer than a weekend were permitted, and the married men were told to send their wives to wherever they were going to live for the duration. When I told Jean, she cried, and it was then that she told me she wanted a baby. The specter of a widow and child bothered me; however, the Japanese were on the run and this job looked fairly safe, or so I thought. So I didn't say no.

When it came time to load the ship, the 51st Battalion became a beehive of activity, full of excitement and trepidation. We said our last good-byes, and all leave of any kind was cancelled. We had no idea where we were going or the exact day of departure. They were kept secret because of the chance enemy submarines would get the word. Finally, one evening during the last week of August, we shoved off. The ship was absolutely crammed with our 1,100 men plus about half of our construction equipment. The other half was being carried by an amphibious combat ship called an LST (Landing Ship Tank), which had gone on a few days ahead of us because it was too slow to stay with our big convoy.

The convoy was designed to protect trans-ocean ships from enemy submarines during wartime. It consisted of a group of transport and cargo ships having fairly equal cruising speeds which allowed them to sail together in formation, surrounded by several Navy destroyer escorts. The destroyer escort was a relatively small, very fast, light warship designed and equipped to locate, chase, and destroy submarines. It was armed with deck guns to fire on subs caught on the surface, and depth charges to sink those submerged, thus the name destroyer.

It was my first trip in a convoy, and whenever I had time, I stood leaning on the rail in total fascination. A convoy is beautiful, whether seen from a deck or the sky. The inner core of ships sailing in several parallel columns are never equally spaced, for each has her own individuality. One is always straggling or ranging ahead until the convoy commander becomes irritated and signals, "Ahoy! So & So. Take station! Keep station!" The screen of destroyer escorts surrounding the transports are like a loose jointed necklace—the beads lunging to port or starboard and then snapping back to center with great water sprays around the bow. Each destroyer is nervous, questing like a hunting dog in the field. All eyes are topside, looking for the enemy. Below, the submarine sound gear listens for him. On the sea surface, the radar antenna feels for him ahead. When sailing at night, only a few ships, a little darker than the black water, can be discerned. The convoy master has to consult the radar screen to ascertain that his flock is all there.

Although members of the 51st Construction Battalion were technically passengers on board the ship, we were still expected to help the ship's crew by performing certain duties. All of our officers and CPOs were required to stand watches—four hours on duty, eight hours off—around the clock. There were several types of duty and numerous watch stations. One of the most important watch stations was at the entrance of each hold billeting enlisted men, where a couple of chiefs kept law and order, watched for fires, and prevented fights. Another important watch station was on the upper decks where first class mates were posted to look for signs of submarines and torpedoes. The officers stood duty as officers of the day or supervised the petty officers on watch.

Each time I went topside for the dawn watch, it was always a wonder to see the same ships day after day, each in her appointed station, each with her characteristic bow wave, lifting and dipping, ever the inevitable straggler and the inveterate smoker; and out a mile or so, the greyhounds of-the-sea—our destroyer escorts—ceaselessly hunting.

Aboard ship the enlisted men were quartered in holds below the main deck in the after-half of the ship. Each hold was like a windowless warehouse divided by walls and each had a separate entry topside. Bunks were tiered six high along narrow aisles, leaving just room to lie down, with no place for men to sit. The spaces were not air-conditioned, but were ventilated with pipes leading to open air on the main deck where large tuba-like horns could sweep up the wind. Even so, these quarters turned out to be great sweat boxes. To make things more difficult, many men got seasick, which in turn made others sick.

All hands were permitted to go topside to wander around the decks and even to sleep there. However, the decks were jam-packed with heavy construction equipment, jeeps, boxes, and a variety of cargo which made it almost impossible to find a place to lie down or even to sit comfortably. Because of all the equipment, emergency aid and disembarking drills were crazy, and exercise areas were non-existent. Throughout the war, the men on board in these conditions believed in a myth that the situation had been purposely planned because the Navy wanted everyone infuriated by the time they hit the beach.

Down below in the holds, the men were quiet, though awake, writing letters, playing cards, rummaging through their packs and sea bags, reading, or just talking. Their bunks were littered with helmets, helmet liners, knapsacks, entrenching tools, canteens, bayonets, first-aid kits, packs of cigarettes, web belts, C-rations, ponchos, and various items of clothing. On deck men lined the rail and milled around, bored and frustrated, the best they could.

To avoid confusion, the enlisted men were served their meals cafeteria style. They lined up according to company and platoon and were allowed fifteen minutes to sit at a mess hall table and eat their food. The plan kept two lines moving so everyone could be fed in about an hour and a half. Enlisted men ate mainly corned beef hash, navy beans, potatoes, bread, coffee, apples, butter, and jam. In spite of all the discomfort, morale was high. There were few fights and good discipline.

The officers were billeted in state rooms above the main deck. These were also sweat boxes, but at least they weren't crowded and the officers had their own deck to sleep on. I rated a single room with a porthole, which was relatively good. We had our meals in an officer's mess and were served meat, potatoes, canned vegetables, coffee, bread, and a pastry dessert. When we weren't having meals, the mess room was converted into a lounge which was well supplied with reading material and fresh, strong, coffee. After about eight days the convoy stopped at Pearl Harbor and disbanded. Though we were in port a couple of days, no one was allowed to go ashore except Commander Smith, who went to Navy headquarters to get our sealed orders. The next day, we joined another convoy and sailed out of Pearl Harbor. The orders weren't divulged to us until we were back at sea, headed for our destination.

That noon at mess, Commander Smith called for a meeting as soon as the food was cleared. "Gentlemen, please sit down." Then he announced, "We're going to Ulithi Atoll in the Caroline Islands." He unfolded a large map of the Pacific, hung it on the bulkhead, and pointed to a tiny speck due east of the Philippines and directly north of New Guinea, about 10 degrees above the equator.

Ulithi Atoll is a string of tropical coral islands encircling a lagoon of about twenty miles in diameter. The lagoon is deep enough to moor any size ship and has two narrow channels for ships to pass in and out easily and safely. The Pacific fleet planned to use Ulithi Atoll as a rendezvous and staging area for future attacks on Japan. Our task was to build an all-purpose air station on the island named Falalop, the largest island in the chain. This island was about a mile long at its widest point and an average elevation of about six feet above high tide.

The 51st Battalion was directed to build at least a usable airstrip within three weeks after they landed. Bill Towner (Lt. CEC, USNR Company D Commander) was assigned this task. At the same time, a floating boat dock, fuel storage facilities, and all necessary roads were to be constructed by my Company A. The Battalion also would have to build two camps: one for ourselves and another to service 100 aviation personnel. Hinkley (Lt. CEC, USNR, Company C Commander) and Marshall (Lt. CEC, USNR, Company B Commander) were to build these. Each project manager was

Falalop, the largest island in the Ulithi Atoll chain, after the 51st Batallion completed its work. Note the airstrip, roads, and dock (*upper right*).

to choose his own staff, men and equipment and prepare detailed construction plans immediately upon landing. If there were still Micronesian natives on the island, we were to leave them strictly alone. They would eventually be removed to another island by the Navy.

Up to this time, the voyage had been very routine, but that night at about 0200 the ship's siren screamed, sounding general quarters. It meant that everyone must put on life jackets, the ship's crew must report to their battle stations, and the passengers down in the hold must get on deck. It also meant enemy submarines were in the area. A warrant officer and I quickly got dressed and rushed to the entrance of the hold where our company was billeted. By this time our platoon leaders had the men pouring on deck, stepping on life vests and climbing over the cargo, trying to be as close as possible to their assigned life boat. Members of the ship's crew stood by the life boats, ready to lower them at the proper signal.

The maneuver went surprisingly well. The crowd, however, was quiet and apprehensive, not the usual laughing, shouting jostling bunch. Several men asked me if this were a drill. I told them that it wasn't, but I was wondering the same thing myself. Then it happened—there was a great orange flare followed by a muffled roar. A torpedo had hit the ship steaming off our starboard quarter. Fortunately it turned out to be a freighter, not a troop transport. Guns cracked at imaginary targets, star shells broke out, and the convoy kept its zigzag, evasive course. In the distance we could hear the rumbling of depth charges exploding under water and knew that, although we couldn't see them, the destroyer screen was frantically and relentlessly trying to locate the responsible submarine.

Everyone aboard experienced a helpless fury and dread. There could be a German-type wolf pack with a number of enemy subs lying in wait ahead of us. We passed the burning ship, which sat dead in the water, and watched the glow as it disappeared behind us. Later we were told the ship sank, but the crew had been rescued. There was no report as to what happened to the sub that torpedoed it. It probably got away.

TWENTY-ONE

Ulithi Atoll

G RADUALLY THE WEATHER GREW WARMER, AND THE tropical sunsets which glowed from behind cloud formations became more beautiful. It was warm enough to sleep on deck, and after dinner the men scrambled to find places. One thing they couldn't do on deck was smoke because the flare from a cigarette lighter could be seen through the periscope of a lurking submarine. I hauled my bedding up to the officer's deck every night for the rest of the voyage.

Early on the morning of September 23, we crowded on deck as we approached Ulithi. What we saw appeared to be groves of coconut trees floating in the water. As we grew closer, we could see the surf slapping at the thin line of white coral which formed the island under the trees. We went south along the eastern shore, then turned west and entered a huge lagoon with coconut tree-covered islands forming a great circle around us. We were the only ship in the harbor.

We had been assured that Marine Rangers had swept each island for enemy soldiers before we arrived. The first of our people to go ashore, of which I was one, were the beach master's party. Our job was to quickly explore the lagoon side of the island and decide where the men and equipment could best land. When we arrived at a decision, we set up large posts with flags at the top to give the landing boats direction.

While this was going on, the small landing boats, which had been carried on the ship's deck, were lowered over the side into the sea. They each held fifty men and were like regular steel tubs with ramps which could be let down when the boat beached. Most of our heavy equipment was carried by a similar, but larger landing craft (LCTs or Landing Craft Tank) which had joined the convoy in Honolulu and sailed with us.

As soon as all personnel were landed, we selected company camp sites, set up pup tents, and chowed down on cold C-rations. It took several days to get everything organized: our house tents up, mess facilities functioning, and the work assignments started. When I look back I realize how really very well organized we were. We were in operating condition in three days; except of course, we were still sleeping on the ground and eating cold, dry food. Under circumstances other than war, Falalop was a south sea island of dreams: palm trees gently swaying in the wind, beautiful vines and wild flowers of every description, few mosquitoes, lots of birds, and no reptiles or land animals, except for some rats and harmless six-foot long tree lizards. Best of all was the balmy weather, wonderful swimming and skin diving, and the marvelous tropical sunsets that blazed in the western sky, always with the skyline of a great city formed by towering black clouds stretched on the horizon. Every evening I watched that sunset. No place in the world could be more different from the dank, dark, forbidding atmosphere of Guadalcanal and the Melanesian Islands.

When we landed there were Micronesians on the island. These natives lived in exotic hurricane-proof houses with earthen floors, thatched roofs made of palm leaves, and half-walls made of split palm logs. The upper half was left open so the breeze could provide natural air-conditioning. Each house had a carved frieze around it. The carvings were black dolphins on a white background. (I managed to save a few pieces to send home to Jean for house decorations.) Even though we were told not to fraternize with the natives, we did. We traded watches, knives, matches, and clothing for necklaces, beautiful rare shells, fresh fish, and various artifacts. The Ulithi native life and culture was quite unspoiled by white people. The men wore loin cloths, and the women wore a scarf affair around their waist. It was better for everybody that they moved these people, for the sailors were

The author (*left*) in a jeep on Ulithi.

doing everything they could to get together with the women. Our officers found the situation almost unmanageable, not that they were much better.

After the natives were relocated to another island, we burned all their huts, which I felt very sad about, but they were in the way and full of rats. One day shortly after the natives were moved I found and rescued my best souvenir. It was a one-man outrigger canoe. It was beautifully carved out of palm wood and painted orange with white and black native hieroglyphs, just like in the magazine ads for Hawaii. I loved it and paddled around in it whenever I had any extra time. I tried to send it home, but for some reason my grandmother wouldn't accept it when it was delivered.

While the huts were being burned and the camps built, the airplane runway was cleared of palm trees, which I requested to be saved for use in

The author with his rifle on Ulithi.

constructing a dock. After the runway was cleared, we discovered that there was a swampy area rather like quick sand in the center of it. This area couldn't be drained.

Lieutenant Towner, Commander Smith, and Lt. Montgomery were perplexed. As I listened to them talk about the swamp problem in a construction meeting, I thought of my Grandfather McCandless. He was a blasting expert and had obtained his experience from years of hard-rock

Officers' quarters for the 51st Construction Batallion, Ulithi.

mining and highway construction in the mountains. Because I was interested, he'd spent many hours instructing me on the various techniques of blasting, and I witnessed many of his jobs. Then I remembered how he had solved a problem comparable to this one. I spoke up and described what we could do: lay dynamite in the swamp; pile up a large amount of coral in the shape of a big pyramid over the dynamite area; then shoot. The mud would blow out around the perimeter of the pyramid at ground level and the piled coral would fill the hole and raise the elevation so that the water would be drained away in ditches.

Smith was an office building engineer; Montgomery was an ocean dredger; and Towner worked for a utility company. They really knew nothing about blasting and decided it was a crazy idea. Towner, whom I didn't get along with anyway, seemed offended and called me stupid, which made me mad and would have caused a fistfight if Montgomery hadn't grabbed me by the arm and pulled me down. Finally, Commander Smith, not knowing what else to do, decided to try my idea. To everyone's astonishment, it worked like a charm.

From then on I was the 51st Battalion blasting officer. I was later somewhat sorry for this because a few days later Smith called me into his office tent and told me I was to be loaned to the 71st Seabees for a few days to help them solve some blasting problems. He said a PBY aircraft would pick me up to take me 400 miles south to Peleliu, where the 71st was located. Smith, the son-of-a-bitch, had volunteered me. The big problem was that the battle to control Peleliu was still going on with the Japanese. Our Marines had captured the airfield, but not the rest of the island.

TWENTY-TWO

Peleliu

THE PALAU ISLANDS LIE ABOUT HALF WAY BETWEEN THE Marianas and the Philippines, which are 1,500 miles apart, and are so remote that none of the colonial powers ever bothered to develop them. Peleliu is the southern-most island in the Palau group. The United States wanted to capture these islands because they believed them to be the key to the Japanese defense of the surrounding atolls through which General MacArthur's armies must pass on their drive to Mindanao, the large island at the southern end of the Philippines.

Because of lack of intelligence information concerning the Palau Islands, the United States Navy mistakenly assumed Peleliu would be easy to take. There were no maps of the island nor were there any coast watchers or former residents to advise them as to what they could expect. The only intelligence information came from the Navy frogmen and submarine shore parties, neither of which could see inland.

For some reason, the aerial photographs were interpreted to indicate the island was flat. The fact was that Peleliu, seven miles long and two miles wide, was covered with jagged limestone ridges running the length of the island and overlooking a Japanese airstrip, which had to be captured immediately to control the island. The heights, which the Japanese had turned into fortresses by installing underground tunnels, were virtually impervious to air and naval bombardment. One hulk of rock, christened "The Point" by the Marines who had to take it, rose thirty feet above the water's edge—a bastion of huge fractured boulders, deep gorges, and razor-sharp spikes, the entire mass studded with pill boxes reinforced with steel and concrete.

A great spiny ridge of rock known as Umbrogal, until the Marines christened it "Bloody Nose Ridge," dominated the beaches upon which the Americans had to land. It was steep, heavily forested, and riddled with caves. The enemy knew that any assault on the Peleliu would have to hit the mushy white sand on the southern coast because the airfield was there and the reef was close to the shore, allowing assault boats to almost land on the beach. It was the misfortune of the attackers, the United States Navy and Marines who made up the 3rd Amphibious Force, that the Japanese commander decided not to meet the Marines on the beach with the usual banzai charges, which exposed their men to our overwhelming fire. He chose instead to fight using the murderous Japanese doctrine of attrition, which meant that they remained in their camouflaged caves and from the entrances rained cannon and machine gun fire down upon the attacking Americans. From the beach, the Americans blasted away with their artillery and tanks, but they were unable to substantially hurt the Japanese. The caves, which housed thousands of Japanese soldiers, were virtually impenetrable.

They had sliding steel doors protecting the entrances and were well-stocked with food and ammunition. The Japanese positions and tactics put up a very effective defense which killed thousands of Americans in only a few days. Slowly but surely, however, the Marines climbed to the cave entrances where they sprayed the enemy with flame throwers and threw in TNT satchel charges.

By the time I arrived on Peleliu, the airfield was supposed to have been secured, although the fighting still continued about a mile away. I say "supposedly" secured because it turned out that a few caves which sheltered the enemy and overlooked the airfield had been missed.

Upon landing on Peleliu, I inquired about the location of 71st Seabee

The airfield on Peleliu.

headquarters, then headed up the beach in the direction indicated. As I progressed, I saw the smoldering remains of destroyed vehicles and burned out tanks littering the recent battle field. About a quarter of a mile behind the flat land stood Bloody Nose Ridge, where cave entrances ringed by black soot left by flame throwers were visible. Everywhere between the beach and the ridges stood topless, shattered, burned out palm trees. The whole vista was like a scene from the *Inferno*. Nearby, a battery of American 105 MM howitzers was banging away, and in the distance I could hear explosions and see a wall of grey-black smoke covering the far side of the island where the fighting was still going on.

I found the headquarters of the 71st Battalion, a tent surrounded by a coral revetment, located in a grove of trees on the beach. Inside, I was greeted by a haggard and disheveled lieutenant commander who turned out to be the executive officer. He said the original plan was for the Marines to secure the island in four days, and accordingly the Seabees had landed on the third day with orders to go to work immediately to restore the existing Japanese airstrip. Instead, however, the battle had been going on for almost two weeks, and the island still wasn't secure.

The Seabees had not been able to work on the strip, but spent their time doing combat engineering tasks for the Marines. When the airfield had been secured, the Seabees' first job was to extend its north end, which ran into a swamp. They were faced with the same problem that had confronted the 51st Battalion on Ulithi: how to dry up the swamp so they could build a solid base which airplanes could use. Since nobody on board knew a thing about blasting, or highway building for that matter (the CO and XO were both house builders), they wired their Brigade for help. The Brigade contacted the 51st who, in turn, sent me.

The executive officer said we could wait to check out the problem the next morning because it was beginning now to get dark. He found me a vacant tent, gave me a canteen of water, and showed me the chow wagon, a trailer with a canvas canopy. It contained several five-gallon cooking kettles, all emanating odors of cooking corned beef hash, which was more than welcome after the cold, dried, capsulated C-rations I'd been living on. I filled my helmet with water, washed my hands and face, and went back to headquarters tent, where I'd been invited to share a bottle of Old Grandad with the executive officer before dinner. As I remember, that whiskey tasted pretty good.

That night, tired as I was, I couldn't get any sleep because of the whoom-whoom-whoom of the nearby howitzers shelling the enemy on the other side of the island. Once in a while enemy guns returned the gun fire, knocking down trees, starting fires, and creating more craters on the airstrip. In the north, over Bloody Nose Ridge, I could see the red-orange glare of fire and hear the rumble of war-like continuous thunder.

The next morning, accompanied by a squad of fifteen Marines each armed with a Thompson submachine gun, the Executive Officer, the Operations Officer, a few chief petty officers, and I walked the length of the airstrip, staying concealed in the trees on the side opposite Bloody Nose Ridge. We camouflaged ourselves the best we could with palm fronds. After an hour of hacking our way through the vines and undergrowth in terrible humid heat, we arrived at our destination—the swamp at the north end of the field. It was big, maybe 300 feet long, much larger than the big mud hole we'd encountered on Ulithi. I estimated we'd need a ton of

Marines move through the trenches on the beach during the battle on Peleliu Island.

dynamite, or its equivalent in TNT shaped charges, and 2,000 tons of coral. After I briefly described how I proposed to do the job and explained the theory of sequential detonation, we turned to retrace our path back to headquarters.

Suddenly from across the airfield, a couple of Nambus (Japanese light machine guns) opened up over our heads. I knew they were Nambus by the high pitched burps—sort of like wood peckers—that I'd heard at Guadalcanal. The bullet streams were passing over our heads. I'm sure they couldn't see us, but they knew we were there. In a moment they lowered their aim. The bullets spattered palm tree trunks and broke off limbs and big chunks of wood. Automatically, we threw ourselves prone on the ground and crawled behind trees. Then came rifle shots whirring overhead from the enemy. The Marine sergeant yelled that he thought this preceded a banzai charge eventually from across the airfield and that he'd position his fifteen men with their Tommy guns where they could shoot anyone trying to cross the bare expanse. We Navy people were to retreat away from the airfield to the beach and try to work our way home. He'd already radioed for help, but it would be a while coming. We were armed only with hand guns and three grenades each—not a very effective defense in this situation.

Then it came. Suddenly, there was yelling and screaming. What must have been fifty Japanese riflemen, bayonets leveled, leaped out of the jungle on the other side of the airfield and started running towards us. I don't think they could see us even then, but there was no doubt that it was one of their famous banzai charges. I turned and ran from tree to tree, back to the front line. It looked to me like it would be better to stay and help fight, even with a .45 automatic and three hand grenades. If the Japanese broke through the Marine defense, we'd be bayoneted in the back trying to escape. When the on-coming Japanese were about 100 feet from us, the sergeant ordered, "Fire!" Fifteen Thompsons opened up; the Japanese dropped like bricks. I guess they hadn't really located us—just a mindless charge against what they thought was an American patrol.

Two Japanese got through the fire and raced straight toward me. Again, I don't think they saw me because I was behind a tree and on the ground. When they were about thirty feet from me, I dropped them both with my Colt 45, a vicious weapon up-close because it threw a half-by-one-inch lead slug 1,000 feet per second. It not only stopped them; it knocked them over backwards, which is just what this gun was designed to do. It was a close call, and I was trembling. Talk about adrenaline running and combat highs, I was feeling almost drunk.

Our group suffered no casualties, and all the Japanese were dead, lying in every grotesque position imaginable. We reloaded our weapons, sank back in the brush, regrouped, and headed for home, leaving the bodies where they were. On the way, we encountered the platoon coming to our rescue. In the dense foliage, it could have been a dangerous situation had our sergeant not kept in close radio contact with them so that they wouldn't mistake us for the enemy. That was one long morning.

I spent the next few days designing my swamp blasting project, wrote some letters, and waited for the Marines to really mop up the south end of the island. This they did by laboriously going through all the caves, sealing the entrances of those that might shelter small groups of hold-outs, while American F4U Corsair fighters dropped napalm fire bombs on any other areas where the enemy might be hiding.

The day finally came when it was deemed safe to start work on the airstrip. The enemy howitzers, which had kept the field plowed up, were silent, and surprise enemy patrols like we had encountered were no longer on the prowl. Upon getting clearance, I gathered my demolition team and the TNT shape charges, loaded up two track personnel vehicles, and went out to the swamp. This time we rode down the airfield. By the end of a sixteen-hour day, we were able to blast, and the plan worked very well. The next day, I scrambled aboard the PBY supply plane, which flew on to several other islands. In a couple of days, I was back on Ulithi after quite an adventure.

The author (*left*) and fellow officers driving across the floating bridge constructed by the 51st Batallion on Ulithi.

TWENTY-THREE

Back on Ulithi

I N MY WEEK'S ABSENCE, THE BATTALION HAD GOTTEN QUITE a bit of
work done. The airfield had been completely cleared and grubbed,
a coral quarry had been started; and full-sized tents for our living quarters
had been erected. But best of all we had hot food and good messing
facilities. Our big portable food freezers were in operation, enabling us
to pick up frozen meat and other frozen food from ships that came into
the lagoon. My executive officer, Lt.(jg) "Texas Jim" Gay, had done a
fine job organizing our company to undertake the assigned work.

I immediately started work on construction of the road network and the
floating dock and erection of the prefabricated steel fuel tanks. Already, it
was nearing the second week in October, and we had to have all the basic
facilities completed by the mid-October. To accomplish this feat we
worked twenty-four hours a day, all hands working a twelve-hour shift.

Building the fuel tanks and roads was routine, just a lot of work; the fun
was in building the dock, which had been left to me. The only useful
materials we brought with us were some large 5' x 10' x 5' steel pontoons.
The rest we had to improvise. I designed the dock in two sections. The first
section was stationary and about 200 feet long, starting at road level on the
beach and extending fifty feet across the beach to the water's edge. It then

extended the other 150 feet out through the surf to a point where the water was about ten feet deep and not too turbulent. This section was made of palm tree logs layered over each other in equilateral triangles, tied together at the corners with 5/8" steel reinforcing bars used as giant pins. Each triangular structure formed a caisson. They were floated into place and sunk, forming a huge honey comb which was then filled with coral from a quarry I had set up. All together it formed a level 150 foot road above high tide. However, there was a difference of six feet between high and low tide. At low tide even small boats were unable to dock. To solve the problem, I added a 20' X 100' floating dock comprised of the hollow steel floating pontoons tied together with steel channels and fastened at one end to the coral dock with an improvised cable hinge.

Although Commander Smith was delighted, he said not one complimentary word to me. The job was a good experience: not only had I completely engineered and built a successful waterfront structure requiring considerable improvisation, but I had learned a great deal about underwater blasting. I had done all the diving and the setting and shooting of the TNT shape charges, a high explosive which leveled off the ocean bottom to receive the caissons. This job, together with the swamp blasting, established and typed me, as far as the battalion commander was concerned, as a waterfront engineer specialist.

The fact was that I really knew very little about waterfront construction; it was just that no other Seabee officer around there knew anything about it. I loved it! It was exciting. It was true that Executive Officer Lt. Montgomery had been a dredging engineer in civilian life, but he had no experience with blasting. Also, he had wanted to try something different, so he hadn't told the Navy about his previous experience. They probably wouldn't have paid any attention to it anyway, the way they assigned people was sometimes irrational.

One morning, I awakened at my usual time, 0500, put on a jockey strap, and headed for the beach 100 yards away to take my morning swim. As I emerged from the palm trees and looked across the lagoon, I could hardly believe my eyes. It was full of war ships—all sizes and types. Aircraft carriers, battle ships, cruisers, tankers, destroyers, ten or twelve submarines,

Completed floating dock addition.

etc. all riding peacefully at anchor. They had slipped in during the night. I have no idea how they could have done it so silently, and I realized then why we were on Ulithi. It was a great protected hiding place into which the big powerful American task forces could rendezvous. There was nothing like it closer to Japan until we took the Philippines.

The next day at parade we were told that Admiral Halsey was going to visit us and inspect our work, which had been completed on time. I was told to be at the dock and stand at the top of the ladder to help the boarding party on deck, which was standard naval etiquette. Commander Smith, Lt. Montgomery, and Lt. Towner were to stand back and act as the receiving party.

At the appointed time, we could see the Admiral's gig (speed boat) plying across the lagoon. It pulled up to our dock; the lines were thrown up to secure it; then the Admiral began to climb the ladder. Just as he reached the top, he missed his hand-hold. I quickly reached over and grabbed him by the arm (which was the purpose of my being there). He didn't say a word; he just climbed up onto the dock and spat out a big cud of chewing tobacco, most of which landed on my shoes. Again he said nothing.

He walked over to the receiving party, shook hands, and said, "I like this fucking-good dock. Who built it?"

"The 51st Battalion, Sir," Commander Smith replied.

"I know that, for Christ's Sake! Who built it?" he asked again.

"It was a joint effort, Sir," the Commander answered.

"What Officer was in charge?"

"Lt. McCandless, Sir," Smith replied.

"McCandless, come over here." Halsey looked at me for the first time and smiled. "Fine job!" Then turning to the receiving party, he said, "Send him over with his working party tomorrow. I want a dock like this on Asor."

"Yes, Sir," Smith replied, looking very irritated. I'm sure that as the battalion commander he expected to get the credit, and I think he probably should have.

The next three weeks I spent commuting back and forth in a whale boat between Ulithi and Asor—supervising the dock crew on Asor and as well as my other projects on Ulithi.

About the middle of October, the day after the airstrip was completed, a Marine air group moved in. Their job was to guard the ships moored in the lagoon. The air group was equipped with F6F fighters (Hell Cats), F2U fighters (Corsairs), TBF torpedo planes (Avengers), and a squadron of SB2C dive bombers (Hell Cats.). I had been away from flying now for two years, and these planes were all new to me. It was amazing how much naval aviation had advanced primarily in speed, armament (rockets), tactics, night flying, instrumentation, and radar—I had come from the dark ages.

I could hardly wait to get acquainted with some of the flyers, and have an opportunity to fly in the new planes. Of course, I couldn't ride in the single-seat fighters, but I could in the others. With the help of a couple of bottles of whiskey and some beef steak, which we Seabees had and the Marines didn't, I soon made friends. Marines and Seabees got along well anyway because they needed each other. But in any event, I got lots of rides and chances to handle the planes' controls in the air.

The Avenger was a huge, fast, heavy, powerful torpedo bomber that carried a crew of three. It wasn't very maneuverable and was heavy on the controls, but very stable and pleasant to fly. The Curtis Hell Cat dive bomber, however, was the opposite; fast and powerful, but unstable, tricky, and had nasty stall characteristics. According to the Marines, it was even hard to hold on target in a dive. They named it "the beast" and "widow-maker." This plane never did replace the Dauntless, which supposedly it was designed to do.

The best friend I made among the Marine flyers was a stocky Polish kid from New Jersey named Pete Stokowski. Often after dinner, we'd take walks along the beach and watch the beautiful tropical sunsets and talk about what we were going to do when the war was over. Pete had gone to Amherst College before joining the Marines, and he planned to go to law school when he got out of the Corps. Pete was on his first tour of duty since flying school, and he was piloting an Avenger.

One afternoon, Pete invited me for a short hop in the Avenger before dinner. He wanted to check out some repairs recently made on the plane. I couldn't go because I was on duty as Security Officer of the Day. But I watched him take off alone: he roared down the strip and climbed to about 500 feet, then suddenly went into a vertical nose dive and crashed head-on into the reef. I could see the airplane tail standing vertically in the air as the surf washed around the fuselage. (Lady Luck was still with me.)

The ambulance immediately took off down the runway to get him. I didn't go down to see them pull Stokowski out of his craft because pilots, or ex-pilots like me, never visit crashes. Instead, I walked sadly up to the field hospital in case he was alive when they brought him in. If he survived the crash, I knew he would be badly hurt. But when they brought him in, he was dead—nearly every bone in his body broken. I was the first to officially identify him because I happened to be there. A couple of weeks later I wrote to his mother and fiance and sent them some pictures.

In thinking it over, I decided that probably two-thirds of our aviators were killed on operational or training flights, not in combat—some little pilot error or a faulty engine. I concluded that I wouldn't have missed flying for the world, but now I was better off being a Seabee.

Pontoon dock breaking up during the typhoon.

TWENTY-FOUR

Typhoon

TOWARD THE END OF NOVEMBER WE RECEIVED STORM WARNINGS. An especially violent hurricane was sweeping across the central Pacific and was predicted to hit Ulithi in a matter of hours. It was reported to be so violent that the entire fleet moored in the Ulithi lagoon weighed anchor and left to ride out the 100-mile-an-hour winds at sea.

We on the island had little protection. Waves could sweep across the reef and probably even across the entire island. The best precautions we could take were to park all our heavy equipment and machinery in the center of the island, pull our boats ashore, wear a helmet to protect ourselves from flying coconuts, and be prepared to tie ourselves to palm trees, if necessary. We also stored our canned food, ammunition, records, files, tools, water, and personal gear under well-tied down tarps on the seats and tops of the heavy equipment. The big dump trucks and bull dozers were particularly useful. By the time we got everything in place, the shrieking wind was making the palm trees bow half way to the ground and throw coconuts at us like cannon balls from sling shots. Soon the waves came crashing over the reef, covering the entire beach to the edge of the trees. I ran down to the boat dock just in time to see the floating steel-pontoon causeway come apart on the crest of a twenty foot wave. It was obvious that the caisson dock would follow. I then went over to the beached boats to check their tie-downs. After what I'd just seen, I didn't think they were pulled up high enough onto the beach. I went back to headquarters and reported my opinion and what I'd just seen to the captain. He agreed and directed me to muster a detail with a couple of bull dozers and pull the boats farther up the beach.

Once the boats were secured, I decided I'd better get something to eat because it was going to be a long, wet, cold night. I found the officer's mess cook who gave me a can of Van Camp pork and beans, two tins of sardines, and a cup of coffee. I took my rations and joined a group of officers wearing Navy oil skins and ponchos, sitting on the ground, eating. They also had a couple of bottles of whiskey. So we ate and drank, waiting out the storm. Suddenly, there was a great clap of thunder and the light rain turned to a cloud burst. Torrents of rain, propelled by what must have been a sixty mile-an-hour wind, came at us horizontally, rather than vertically. But the fury of the tropical hurricane (known as a typhoon in the tropics) still hadn't really gotten going. Soon the waves breaking over the reef became large enough to sweep the whole island, each succeeding wave deepening until the water came almost up to our knees. With the howling wind, the crashing of the waves, and the noise of the wildly swinging palm trees, communication among people became almost impossible.

It was scary because there really wasn't any way for us to escape and it was the first time in weeks that I was cold. The only thing that prevented us from being swept out to sea and drowning was that we had tied ourselves to the palm trees, which nature designed to survive typhoons. The palm trees broke up the waves and bent with the wind but didn't uproot. The storm raged most of that night, and by morning it had subsided, although it was still dangerous. The captain decided to keep all of our equipment where it was until we were sure we weren't just enjoying a lull—the eye of the storm—and were not going to be zapped again. As it turned out, we had seen the worst. When the weather died down, the ships came back and we surveyed our losses, which were considerable. The airfield was badly torn up; fifty airplanes were ruined; and our camp site, sanitary facilities, and much of our food had been washed away. The roads were impassable, and the dock, of course, was gone. Fortunately, our heavy equipment and tools were okay, and we had enough canned food, water, and fuel to last until the fleet returned and we could re-provision. In any event, we immediately went to work repairing the airfield and roads. The Skipper didn't want to rebuild the dock unless it was absolutely necessary because he suspected that we were due to pack up and leave Ulithi shortly, heading northward toward Japan—maybe to Guam or Saipan.

Just about dawn one morning, we heard an explosion. I didn't think much about it until I noticed our men walking down to the water's edge and looking out into the lagoon. My curiosity piqued, I followed. The men were watching a fleet oil tanker burning at its mooring. The flames were visible, and a huge vertical column of black smoke rose over them. Later, we found out the ship had been hit and hulled by a Japanese kaiten. A kaiten was a human torpedo—one man guiding an especially built torpedo to its target. The man, obviously, had sacrificed his life. The ship eventually sank. Thinking about this incident, it occurred to me that the determination and bravery of the enemy was awesome.

It was now November 20, 1944. We'd been on Ulithi almost two months and away from home three. I missed Jean terribly, but I'd been so busy and tired at night I hadn't had much time to think about it, but when I did it was at sunset time—the half hour every night when I watched the greatest light show on earth.

The first week of December we got the word we were moving north toward Japan. Exactly where we were going, we didn't know. Ulithi was no longer important. The plan was that four LSTs (landing ship tanks) would each carry a construction company and all its equipment. The headquarters company would load with D company (Lt. Towner, Company Commander). Each company commander would run his own show. We figured it would take one day for one company to load, since we could load only one LST at a time. We'd start loading December 14, and company A would be the last one off the beach on December 17, my twenty-seventh birthday. I'd sail four days behind the others.

The LST had a square bow which lowered to the ground and formed a huge ramp when the ship was beached. Thus, bull dozers, shovels, trucks, and other equipment could be driven directly aboard. When we company commanders had our first planning session, it occurred to me, mainly because I was the waterfront construction officer, that an LST might not be able to cross the reef around the lagoon side of Falalop without hanging up on a high spot. I mentioned the problem to Monty. He nodded and said, "I was just thinking the same thing."

With that, the CO looked at me and said, "McCandless, I want you to take the Duck (a glass-bottom boat we had made) and some swimmers and check the entire reef on the lagoon side to see if we can navigate it." The next day we examined the reef and decided there was no way we could beach an LST, no matter how much blasting we might do to make a path. The ship just drew too much water when it was loaded. Now this meant that the LST had to stand about a half mile off shore while we shuttled back and forth with the small LCTs (landing craft tanks) which could only carry one item of heavy equipment at a time.

From then until embarking time the four company commanders spent their time packing, planning, and dividing up the equipment and tools among the companies. As we approached our departure date, the weather began to deteriorate—wind, constant rain, and high surf. The captain began to worry that we might not be able to get off the island on time.

None of us had ever really dried out since the typhoon. Our shoes, clothes and personal belongings were wet and mildewed, and our feet and legs were covered with rash, peeling skin and some kind of fungus like athlete's foot, only much worse. We needed some sunshine and dry days, but they weren't forthcoming. To add to our problems, we hadn't had hot food or mail for a month. A general malaise and deep depression beset the entire battalion.

On December 13, the four LSTs which were to pick us up arrived and asked us to send out a representative to discuss the operation. They wanted to start loading at 0500 the next morning. The surf was very high, almost like it was during a storm. When Commander Smith visited the senior LST officer to make plans, he advised him that we probably shouldn't load until the surf was down. When Smith returned, he was furious. "We start loading tomorrow morning, or they'll go off and leave us!" he told us.

It took Company D from 0500 to midnight to get off the beach. Landing boats turned over, dropping their loads which had to be dragged out of the surf and reloaded; motors flooded; stores got lost in the surf; and some men were hurt. Finally company D was loaded. A short time later Company B started loading, and they took until midnight to finish. Then Company C loaded. At this point I hadn't slept for forty-eight hours, and then it had been a nervous, fitful four hours sleep under a wet tarp. Finally, the fourth day, Company A—my boys—got the go-ahead. It was an advantage to be last because we had learned a great deal from the others' mistakes and the surf was down somewhat.

We spent most of that day loading the heavy stuff, one LCT at a time. Finally, at about 1900. I started sending the men in the small LCVPs (landing craft vehicle and personnel) out to the waiting LST, and at about 2100 the last load left Ulithi. There wasn't room, however, for me and six men. We'd be the last to leave, and I would be the last man off the beach.

I'll never forget the next two hours—waiting at the edge of the surf, standing alone in the rain, cold, soaking wet, dog tired, and so hungry I'd lost my appetite. Up to this time in my life, I'd never been so lonesome or depressed. *What a lousy birthday...twenty-seven years old and what have I got to show for it?* I thought. *Maybe I should have gotten a deferment and stayed safely home and become rich by now.* (In my heart, though, I knew that I belonged where I was.)

At last I saw the searchlight of the boat flashing as it rode the surf onto the sand to pick us up. We waded out waist deep in the water and clambered over the side. I counted everybody and told the coxswain to shove off. Just then, one of the LSTs crewmen asked if I was Lt. McCandless. I acknowledged that I was, and he handed me a bottle of whiskey and said, "Compliments of our captain, Sir." I was surprised and very pleased at this courtesy. I opened the bottle and took a long drink—nothing has ever tasted so good, before or since. I gave each man in the boat one swig and then finished the bottle myself with the last swig. Half an hour later we reached the waiting LST, one of the great products of World War II. I don't remember how big they were, but LSTs were the largest landing ship and the smallest freighter the United States Navy used during the war. They were a sturdy, seaworthy, reliable workhorse.

I was the last man up the ladder. Randolph Keely, a handsome, smiling lieutenant about my age, was at the top to greet me. I saluted the flag and him, then grabbed his hand, and thanked him for the fine reception. He led me to the ward room, where he pulled out another bottle and poured me a glass and handed me my mail. Ten letters from Jean! I was amazed. Randy laughed and said, "If you're anywhere in the world, the Navy'll get it to you. Read your mail, Charlie, then get a hot shower. I'll give you a clean uniform, and we'll have a nice steak dinner. As a matter of fact, I've waited for you, and I'm getting awfully hungry!"

I could hardly believe it, and my morale shot up! I eagerly tore open my letters, the earliest first.

TWENTY-FIVE

Saipan

ON JUNE 13, 1944, THE MIGHTIEST IN FLEET IN HISTORY at that time steamed into the Philippine Sea. It consisted of 112 American warships led by seven battleships and fifteen aircraft carriers carrying nearly 1,000 warplanes. In their midst were 423 transports and freighters loaded with 128,000 fighting men: including the 2nd, 3rd and 4th Marine Divisions, and the 27th Army Division. The mission of the task force was to capture the islands of Saipan, Tinian, and Guam. They were the three largest Mariana Islands, and each was completely encircled by coral reefs, which meant a hard-fought landing.

American control of the large Mariana islands was a vital part of the plan to capture Japan. First, and most important, major Japanese army and navy stations with many airstrips were located on the islands, which if captured by the United States were close enough to Tokyo to be used as bases from which the new American B-29 Super Fortresses could bomb Japan daily. Secondly, Guam had a magnificent anchorage, and the three islands together were large enough to provide an American military staging area for the attack on Okinawa, the last big island to be conquered before the invasion of Japan itself. Thirdly, the three islands were garrisoned with about 70,000 Japanese troops. These could be rushed west across the Philippine Sea to defend the Philippine Islands against General MacArthur's armies, which were fighting north from New Guinea on the left flank of the combined forces, and would soon try to invade the Philippines. To prevent this, these Japanese armies had to be defeated where they were (on the Mariana Islands).

Saipan is a tropical island of luxuriant beauty with rippling green ridges and big valleys. It is about fourteen miles long (north to south), five miles wide, and located about 15 degrees north of the equator. (By comparison, Hawaii is 20 degrees north.) A spine of volcanic mountains, topped by Mount Tipo Pale and the 6000-foot unscalable Mount Topotchau, dominates the interior. To the north and east, the terrain is rugged, angular, flinty, and gnarled by precipitous gorges until it reaches steep limestone and coral cliffs overlooking the sea at Marpi Point, now remembered as Banzai or Suicide Cliff. To the northeast lies Tanapag Plain, where the Japanese had started to build an airstrip and where the 51st Battalion was to camp. In the south of Saipan, the land is more gentle. Terraced hills and fields of sugar cane glide gracefully toward a long level plain. The waters over the reefs are emerald green, and the harbors are sapphire blue and fringed by lovely beaches. On the southwest corner of the island lies Magicienne Bay, which I think is one of the most beautiful tropical spots in the world.

A major part of the interesting story of the invasion and capture of the Marianas was the great air battle of the Philippine Sea, known as "the great turkey shoot." It was four times the magnitude of the battle of Midway and saw the losses of 346 Japanese and 40 American airplanes. Capturing the Mariana Islands cost the lives of 5,500 American and 24,000 Japanese fighting men plus the tragic and unnecessary deaths of thousands of Japanese civilians. The battle lasted from June 15 to August 12, 1944.

****

By the time I arrived on Christmas Day with my A company to join the 51st, Saipan and the other Marianas were securely occupied by American troops. After choosing a camp sight located on a trade

A B-29 Super Fortress on the island of Saipan.

windswept plateau overlooking Marpi Point and the partially built Marpi Point airfield, the 51st Battalion erected an excellent cantonment. The tents were pyramidal and had raised wooden floors to avoid flooding—what luxury! There were two officers in each tent, and my tent mate was Chief Carpenter Ray Manners, the warrant officer of my company. In fact, he was my general construction superintendent.

Among other relatively luxuriant things, we erected a quonset hut for use as an officer's club and furnished it with a bar, cocktail tables, a phonograph, and a marimba (a jazz band musical instrument resembling a xylophone). Each officer donated his weekly booze allowance to the bar, and we assigned a mess boy to be our bartender. From then on we had happy hour every evening before dinner. This was the first time the 51st Battalion had ever been in a location where they could have such luxury. It was interesting to note that when we were in that club we were closer to Japan than were any other allied land-based troops at the time; even so, we were still 1,300 miles away.

By this time the Army Air Force had over 1,000 B-29 bombers, the largest combat aircraft of the war. The B-29s carried a bomb load of 12,000 pounds and were stationed on all three of the big Mariana Islands. Every morning on their way north to bomb Japan, the B-29s flew over us in formation, covering the sky with a great armada: first, flying very high were the planes from Guam, which was 110 miles south of us; next, on a much lower level, maybe a couple of thousand feet, flew the planes from Tinian, twenty miles south; then, almost clipping the tops of the palm trees, roared the planes from Saipan, only eight miles to the south. The noise was absolutely deafening and it shook our tents like a heavy wind.

In the afternoon, however, it was different. The B-29s no longer returned in formation, but were scattered all over the sky, each plane at a different altitude. There were always planes that had one or more of their four engines out. Many times we'd watch them through binoculars: skimming the ocean surface, trying to make it home, then splashing and going under. The search and rescue planes that patrolled the waters all the way from Saipan to several hundred miles north picked up some of the splashers, but our people still lost a great number of men and planes—about twenty planes and 200 men a day.

As officer-in-charge of waterfront construction, I had a large amount of work and a great deal of responsibility. For one thing, I was expected to design as well as build my own structures. Although we were well equipped with basic construction machinery and materials, a great deal had to be improvised. Moreover, the Navy at that time had no standard or prototyped structural designs because the Seabees were a new branch of the service and hadn't yet had time to design them.

The Seabees' motto was "Can Do," and they coined the saying, "We can do the difficult right away, but the impossible takes a little longer." They considered themselves an elite corps, and I think that history proves they indeed were. Every officer had to be a graduate civil engineer, and among those many were experienced contractors. Our capabilities were considered limitless and were taken for granted. For example, I once got this verbal order from the operations officer: "McCandless, Commodore Jones, the harbor master at Garapan, needs a breakwater to shelter his tug boats during stormy weather. Take care of it!" If I had asked the operations officer where I'd get steel sheet piles for the job, he'd have told me not to bother him. He'd say, "Just go find 'em, I'm not your mother."

****

One day I assigned a crew to map the bottom of Magicienne Bay, which was a mile or so from the officer's mess on Aslito Army Air Force (B-29) Base. Since it was noon and I was through with my inspection, I thought I'd pay them a visit and see if they'd let me lunch there. I went in and asked the mess officer, who demurred and said he'd check. When he came back, he smiled and said Wing Commander Colonel Joe Murphy had invited me to lunch with him. I was a little embarrassed at such hospitality, but I followed the mess officer to a table for eight, around which sat six colonels and lieutenant colonels, none of whom were over thirty years old. They were all very polite. The conversation naturally revolved around aviation, but they politely asked me about the Seabees. When we were about to break up, Murphy sighed and said he wished they had construction troops because they badly wanted a tennis court. I thought a minute. Then told him I'd build him one, to just show me where he wanted it. A week later Murphy had two tennis courts. He couldn't believe it.

A few days later a message was delivered to my attention by an Air Force courier. It was from Joe, inviting me to cocktails and dinner. It turned out to be a gala affair given by several B-29 squadrons together. The guests were their own field grade officers (major and up) and a whole bevy of Army nurses—the fly boys always got the girls. I suppose there were seventy or eighty people in attendance. The hors d'oeuvres, champagne, and fresh roast lamb were fabulous. Even the band was great.

After dinner, Murphy called me aside and gave me another invitation. The officers stationed in the air wings at Aslito Air Base owned a house in Brisbane, Australia, which they kept stocked with gourmet food, liquor, and a dozen or so young Australian women. He explained that once a week, supply planes flew down and back, taking officers who'd completed ten missions, for seven days of rest and recreation. He asked if I could get away for seven days and join him in one of these trips. (This explained how they obtained the good party food.) I, of course, declined the offer, but decided that given an attrition rate of forty pilots a day, they deserved everything they could get. The 8th Air Force had it tough in Europe, but probably not any worse than the 20th Air Force in the Pacific. Joe Murphy was killed a week after the party. His plane was shot down over Yokahama. So I guess I couldn't have gone to Australia, anyway.

****

One afternoon I decided to explore a grassy knoll overlooking the cliffs of Marpi Point on the northern tip of the island to see if the rock might be useable for concrete aggregate. Since there were still Japanese hold-outs in the mountains, it wasn't wise to roam around alone; so I got Joe Seims, our disbursing officer, to go with me. We drove my jeep as far as we could, then got out and walked. After walking a few hundred feet, Joe pointed to a little tent-like shelter made of palm leaves. We walked over to see what was in it. The shelter had three sides and a roof, but the north side was open. Propped up inside, facing Japan, was the skeleton of a man wearing the dress uniform of a Japanese general, complete with medals. In his lap was a knife. Joe and I didn't have the heart to take any souvenirs, although those medals were good ones. He had committed suicide rather than surrender, and we respected that.

Saipan had been under Japanese control since 1918. It was the site of a major Japanese army and naval base and was populated by many Japanese farmers and other civilians. When Saipan was invaded, the American troops landed on the south end of the island and drove the enemy north until they were bottled up on the far end where they were expected to surrender. Thousands of civilians were trapped on the north coast along with the soldiers. The Americans pleaded with the Japanese military to surrender, or if not, to at least release the women and children. It was to no avail. The Japanese troops forced the non-combatants over the cliffs to their deaths. Then they made one last, great banzai charge against the Americans until, of course, they were wiped out. Thus, the name Suicide and Banzai Cliffs.

By the time the 51st arrived, the bodies had become skeletons and thousands of human bones and skulls of all sizes, from tiny babies to adults, littered the rocks and beaches at the foot of the cliffs. Our dentist made a collection of skulls, from the smallest to the largest, so he could study them, he said. Some of our enlisted men spent their off-hours prying gold from teeth they found—talk about grave robbers! I understand that today (1988) the Japanese still send annual delegations to Saipan to search for bones to take back to Japan for burial.

One night at about 2200 hours I was sitting in our tent writing letters, and Ray Manners was sitting on his bed reading a book. Suddenly we heard several loud explosions coming from somewhere in camp. We looked at each other and Ray said, "Mac, I think those were hand grenades." I was particularly concerned about such things as hand grenade explosions because I was security officer of the week, which meant I was in charge of our camp perimeter guards. The guards were inspected on a continuous basis by a senior petty officer walking the circle every half hour, and I made the circle every three hours when the guard was changed. Because there were many hold-out enemy soldiers who lived in caves on this end of Saipan and roamed around at night, we kept what we considered very tight security. I answered Ray that I thought the guard ring was tight and the explosions must be something else. Nonetheless, I grabbed three or four hand grenades and my gun and bolted out the door to investigate.

It didn't take very long to discover that, indeed, the noise had been caused by hand grenades which had been thrown into the middle of the outdoor movie amphitheater located on the edge of our camp. The explosion killed several men in the audience and wounded a few others. I headed for the security shack, where an emergency armed patrol automatically assembled in case of trouble. We then all headed to the amphitheater. The ambulance was just arriving, but the audience had dispersed on the run. We spread out and walked up the hill to the guard stations behind the theater. All four guards, who had been posted about 100 feet apart, were dead—stabbed in the kidney, then their throats cut. The barbed wire fence, in front of which they had been standing, had been neatly severed to allow a man to get through—a slick job. There was no point in trying to give chase in the dark (flashlights are targets). Even though only fifteen minutes had passed, the enemy was sure to be far away in their caves by now.

The next day I had a conference with Commander Smith and Lt. Montgomery. We decided to search for near-by caves where the Japanese might be hiding during the day and to seal them off by blowing up the entrances, leaving the Japanese trapped inside to starve. I strongly recommended to Commander Smith that we get professionals to do the job. The 2nd Marine Division was camped five miles away, had nothing to do, and was bored to death. Seabees weren't supposed to fight except to defend themselves in an emergency, and I felt that we weren't properly trained for this type of combat.

But Commander Smith was adamant, "We handle our own problems and by God, you'll do the job! Turn over your construction work to your executive officer and get moving."

I was dismayed and furious, but I had no choice. An infantry officer, I wasn't. I selected thirty suitable men. We had sixty or more satchel charges—canvas bags which each contained six to eight sticks of dynamite taped together with a hand grenade as a detonator. They could be thrown into cave entrances after arming the hand grenades. I armed the men with Garand rifles instead of our usual carbines and got a day's training for all of us from the Marines. I then split the men into three parties who would work separately to search out and blow up caves, but who had orders to stay in touch so we could mobilize for support or retreat if need be. I couldn't get three pack radios, so we used Very signal pistols that shot smoke rockets—red to indicate help was needed; green to indicate retreat to assembly area; yellow to say, "Hold, we are coming." Things went pretty well the first few days, and we blew in a number of caves.

Then one morning it happened. Party number three sent up a red rocket. One of the things the Marines had explained to us was that we could be ambushed easily. An armed enemy party hiding above a cave among the rocks could see us coming before we saw them. They'd have the advantage of surprise and height. I figured that this must have been what happened to party number three and that they were pinned down by fire. The other two parties sent up yellow rockets, telling party number three that we were coming right away. Off we went, each man staying in defilade behind whatever protection he could find.

We soon heard the woodpecker song of a Nambu light machine gun accompanied by occasional rifle fire. I assembled all twenty men from parties one and two and sent a messenger to find the CO of the group in trouble. He was to determine where the machine gun was so we could flank it on both sides. The courier returned and told us that the gun was located well above a cave and protected by several riflemen. Number three party had attempted to attack the cave directly from below and were trapped.

We carefully surrounded the machine gun. Gradually we closed the circle, throwing hand grenades from behind rocks. By twilight we had demolished the nambu and killed all eight of the enemy manning the emplacement. Party number three had lost two men and had several wounded. The hunting expedition was over. Later, Commander Smith was severely reprimanded for this action, and further work of this nature was turned over to the Marines, as it should have been done in the first place.

The USS *Tennessee* firing her 14″/50 main battery guns, as LVTs in the foreground carry troops to the invasion beaches, 1945.

TWENTY-SIX

Iwo Jima

Around the first week of February, 1945, I was called into Commander Smith's office. After a general discussion of how my jobs were going, he said he had a request from the 3rd Seabee Brigade on Saipan for fifteen waterfront men led by an officer, to be assigned temporary duty to undertake a classified (secret) job. He didn't know what the task was, but the men must be good swimmers and have had underwater demolition and mapping experience. Since my A company men were the only Seabees on Saipan who appeared qualified, I was directed to organize a detachment that day. Smith emphasized that this was not a job for volunteers, but only the best men I had. That afternoon I was to report to the headquarters of the 5th Amphibious Force, Prelanding Activities Section.

I drove down to the Saipan naval headquarters and took a shuttle boat to battleship USS *Tennessee* moored in the bay, which was headquarters for Prelanding Activities, 5th Fleet. The officer of the deck gave me permission to come aboard and had me escorted through the enormous ship to an office with a sign on the door that read UDT Unit (Underwater Demolition Teams—Seabee Activity).

The Seabee lieutenant commander on duty invited me to sit down and came to the point immediately: "The 5th Fleet is planning an amphibious attack and is short of UDTs—sixteen-man frogmen teams. They suffered severe losses at Peleliu and Leyte. Have you had any UDT training, McCandless?"

"No, Sir," I answered.

"The Third Seabee Brigade said you were experienced. Explain."

I told him I was involved with waterfront construction and had done underwater work in connection with that. I explained that we were self-taught, had used our own home-made breathing gear, and knew nothing of frogman equipment, methods, or tactics.

"Well, you and your men have a week to learn. Say nothing about this to anyone and get your gang here tomorrow. You will all live on this ship until the mission is over," he said.

When I got back to the 51st, I was upset. Here was another go-around where untrained men were being used for combat missions. UDT Seabees had several months of intensive training and great physical conditioning. We weren't particularly great swimmers; however, we were in good physical condition. I reported back to Commander Smith, gave him the list of the men I wanted, and told him I had no idea when or where we were going. He wished me luck.

The next day my crew and I reported to the same UDT Officer aboard the *Tennessee.* We were told that our job would be to swim the reefs bordering the beaches to be invaded and locate and identify any obstacles such as big rocks, coral heads, and mines or explosive devices that the enemy might have planted underwater for the purpose of damaging or destroying combat landing craft. We would remove these obstacles, using rubber boats to carry the explosives needed for blasting and destroying any dangerous objects. If we found mines, we would be reinforced with crews that were experienced in defusing. All this would be accomplished under the protection of a heavy naval barrage over our heads while we were working. It was anticipated that this task would require two days—the first, for searching out and identifying the objects; the second, for going back and destroying them.

On the first days of training, we were introduced to the equipment we would use, none of which we had ever seen before: black wet suits that covered the torso of the body but did not have long sleeves or leg coverings, a black rubber helmet, fins, masks instead of goggles that we 51st Seabees wore, snorkels, depth indicators worn on the wrist like a wrist watch, a compass, underwater flashlights, a large bowie knife to strap to our leg, and other special paraphernalia which was used in defusing mines and blowing up objects.

For ten days we trained. Twice a day we swam three miles in rough water using the breast stroke. We used the breast stroke because it was less tiring than a crawl and didn't cause splashing that could be observed by the enemy. Speed was not necessary. It was endurance that was needed. To enter the water we sat backwards on the rail of a speeding boat and fell into the ocean feet over head, spacing ourselves in a straight line fifty to seventy-five feet apart. We practiced swimming long distances pushing rubber boats loaded with explosives and then practiced climbing into the boats to get the explosives. We also practiced our recovery after a mission. The recovery was tricky and had to be done correctly or one could dislocate a shoulder. The swimmer faced the bow of a thirty-foot motor boat speeding toward him and held a hand up as a marker until the driver saw him. As the boat passed along side, another man in the boat leaned over the side, rammed his arm onto the swimmer's arm at the arm-pit and hauled him up. As the swimmer swung out horizontally alongside the boat, a second man grabbed his legs to pull him into the boat. In between swims and in the evening, we had chalkboard instruction and slide shows.

Then came the day: February 16, 1945. All shore leave was cancelled and the *Tennessee* moved out. That evening at sea, we were told where we were going, shown aerial photographs, and given charts of the landing beaches at Iwo Jima to study. We were going in to search the beaches at D minus 2, which meant two days before the actual invasion. Every machine gun, mortar, and artillery piece the Japanese defenders had would be ready to shoot us, since they knew we were coming sooner or later. Moreover, they held Mt. Suribachi, a hill which overlooked the landing beaches and provided them a panoramic view. That night I didn't sleep well.

The island of Iwo Jima was a fortified Japanese island about half way between Saipan and Tokyo. We needed possession of this grim island to use as a half-way house for refueling B-29 airplanes coming home from raiding Japan and as a base for Dumbos used to rescue damaged planes that couldn't complete the 1,300 mile run. It could also be used as a base for fighter planes, which were needed to escort the bombers to Japan. The American fighter planes couldn't fly the 2,600 mile round trip from Saipan, but our P-51 and P-47 fighters could fly a 1,300 mile round trip from Iwo— the route which the enemy fighter planes patrolled looking for B-29s.

Iwo Jima is the central island of the Volcano group of the Bonin Islands. It is shaped like a bloated pear four and a half miles long and two and a half miles wide. It was uninhabited except for the Japanese garrison. The northern part of the island is a plateau with rocky, inaccessible shores. At the south end, Mt. Suribachi rises 550 feet above sea level. The beaches extend more than two miles to the north and east from the base of the mountain. These beaches, which are the only place that troop landings can be made, are deeply covered with brown volcanic ash and black cinders which look like sand but are so much lighter than sand that walking is difficult and running is almost impossible.

It was well known to the Americans that Iwo was heavily fortified and would have to be softened up before a landing could be made. Accordingly, the island underwent the most prolonged and disappointing air and navel bombardment of any Pacific island. The Seventh Army Air Force raided it twenty-six times and after November, struck twice daily. Three heavy cruisers bombarded Iwo five times in January, and the B-29s bombed it twice in February. The surrounding islands were also bombed to prevent the Japanese from sending reinforcements, but they did anyway. Some 6,800 tons of bombs and 22,000 rounds of shells, ranging from five to sixteen inches in size, were aimed at Iwo before the invasion.

Unfortunately, Iwo's defenses were of such a nature that neither air bombing nor naval bombardment, no matter how prolonged, could neutralize them. The slopes of Mt. Suribachi contained a labyrinth of dug-in gun positions hiding artillery, mortars, and machine guns. The main feature of the bulbous part of the island, Mt. Suribachi, was an elaborate and intricate network of excavated caves connected by tunnels. In some places there were five levels, each with several entrances. A mortar, machine gun, or other artillery could be set up at the cave mouth, fired a few times, then withdrawn out of sight. Moreover, most of the entrances were camouflaged.

When the Americans started landing, the orders the Japanese commander gave to his men were, "Don't make frontal attacks. Aim at a gradual depletion of the enemy attack forces, and even if the situation gets out of hand, defend the island to the death of every Japanese soldier." And that's the way they fought.

At about 0500 February 17, we were awakened by the roaring of sixteen inch guns and the resulting trembling and rattling of the *Tennessee*. The barrage, without which no swimmer could approach the beach and survive, had started. Eight American battleships, five heavy cruisers, and a flock of destroyers standing a few miles off shore were starting to vigorously shower the south end of Iwo Jima with high explosives for a period of four hours or more, if needed. Hopefully this barrage would prevent the entrenched defenders from getting any opportunity to fire at the swimmers and their accompanying boats.

At about 0530, 105 frogmen organized into seven teams of fifteen each loaded into seven LCI gun boats and headed for the beaches surrounding the base of Mt. Suribachi. All seven boats sailed in a line abreast, spread over about two miles. The plan of action was that when the LCI's arrived at the outer edge of the reef about 1,000 yards off shore, they would unload the frogmen into the water to begin their search. The men would swim directly to the beach in a zigzag fashion staying in parallel lines as far as the breakers on the beach. The LCI would circle on the edge of the reef, waiting to recover the swimmers after about two and a half hours. It was a simple plan, but oh so difficult to accomplish.

By the time we had settled down in the LCI for the seven-mile ride to the reef, we were all on a combat high to the point of trembling. I had to hide my hands so my fifteen men couldn't see them moving. Overhead, the shells from our ships were passing. The shells from five-inch guns whined; the eight-inch guns had a lower pitched whine; the sixteen-inch shells went chug-chug, like a freight train passing. Some shells moaned, some knocked rhythmically; others chirred loudly or rustled tonelessly.

American supplies being off-loaded during the invasion of Iwo Jima.

They fizzled, whined, squealed, or whoofed. The same principle governed all these sounds. The projectiles passing through the air created a vacuum into which the air rushed, but the various sizes, shapes, and trajectories produced different effects.

During the time we rode to the reef, we received no counter-fire from the defenders. It looked like the barrage was really doing its job. (After all, we Americans were supposed to capture Iwo in four days.) As we approached the reef, things changed however. Suddenly, the whole side of Mt. Suribachi, not much more than a mile away, was covered with flickering lights. We couldn't hear anything at first because of the overhead barrage, but we knew the lights were their guns firing. Almost immediately big water spouts appeared around us; then we heard the rat-tat-tat of machine gun bullets bouncing off the steel bow ramp of our LCI. *This barge is going to get blown up,* I thought, and I ordered the men to jump into the ocean immediately. When we were all in the water, the men gathered around me and I signaled them to take their stations. We were to swim in a line abreast, about thirty yards apart, extending from the reef to the shore, thereby swimming parallel to each other. The men were numbered from 1 to 105, which of course included all the frogmen in the attack. The instant our last man was unloaded, our LCI turned a quick 180 degrees and took off as fast as it could to sea.

It was now every man for himself; get to shore, then return to the reef by the appointed time and hope somebody would be there to pick him up. "Maybe all the LCT's would be sunk," I said to myself. I could see one burning already. I decided to worry about that when the time came. My first job was to stay alive and get to the beach and back. The mortars and heavy machine guns were shooting at us, but they were hitting a little behind our line. It seemed that they couldn't see us very well, but that was hard to believe. I hoped nobody in our group would splash around. The wind was coming up, and white caps appeared—that would help. I dove two or three feet below the water surface every few minutes to check the bottom. The visibility was good. The bottom was sandy and littered with small coral heads and rocks. When I reached the surf line, I looked at my watch. We'd been away from the LCT about an hour, so we were on time— in fact, a little ahead of time.

I stopped and looked at Mt. Suribachi. It was enveloped in clouds of grey smoke from the enemy guns and the exploding shells from our barrage. Through the smoke I could still see the pin points of light from machine gun muzzles, the flares of mortars, and now and then a flash of field artillery. All around me, the water spouts of exploding shells continued; each spout shot white-hot pieces of metal in all directions, one tiny piece of which could easily kill a man. Added to this there was still the murderous machine gun fire which steadily swept over my head. I decided the only way I could get any protection was to keep as much of my body under water as possible and still keep swimming.

Since the ocean here at the surf line was fairly shallow and was the most likely place to find obstacles, I made searching dives in a zigzag pattern, but found nothing that would impede a boat landing. I looked at my watch and decided I'd gone shoreward far enough. It was time to get back to be picked up. With the hot gun fire from shore, I realized there was a good chance our people might not be able to get the boats in close enough to recover us—a chilling thought. The planners hadn't anticipated that the enemy could put up and maintain such a deadly defense. Had it not been for the physical and emotional stimulation of the combat high, I would have panicked. I knew that I was in big trouble and I was scared, but I didn't lose my head or lose hope.

I headed back to the recovery area, keeping under water as much as possible until I finally arrived at the outer edge of the reef. The American bombardment of the island was continuing, which was good for us. But there were no recovery boats in sight; however, from an eye level only a foot above the water, my horizon was very short. I felt exhausted and tried to fight off despair by repeating to myself, "They won't let us down, they're coming, they'll keep the faith." I couldn't help remembering, though, that the reason we were here was because the Navy had lost so many of their regulars at Leyte and Peleliu.

I must have treaded water twenty minutes or so when I heard the roar of a fast motor boat. It was a spotter. I raised myself in the water and waved. The boat made a steep turn and circled me. At the same time shooting a parachute flare and dropping a flag float to mark my position. (Although this action may have alerted the enemy to our position, we were so scattered that there wasn't a better way to pick us up.) In no more that ten minutes, the LCI boat appeared on my horizon. I waved at the look-out, and he waved back. I put my arm down by my side and the boat slowed down and slipped expertly by me, then an arm went under mine and I was hauled aboard, flopping down on the bottom of the boat like a fish with several other worn out, but relieved, sailors. We picked up a few more frogmen, then headed for the *Tennessee*.

As we arrived alongside the ship, I could see other LCI's returning. Soon after we were safely aboard the battleship, the heavy barrage stopped and we took off for Saipan. Later that afternoon I was told that out of 120 men who took part in the reconnaissance, seventy-six swimmers and boat crewmen did not return. Of the men lost, six were mine. When I heard this, I couldn't help but cry.

Because none of our people who returned reported any significant obstacles to impede the landing boats, the next day's swim was cancelled, which was fortunate for us because we didn't have enough men left to do a the job successfully. Good luck again!

****

When we returned to the 51st, I immediately checked in with Commander Smith, who was in his tent having his first before-dinner drink. He welcomed me by having his steward pour me a whiskey and soda and inviting me to sit down and tell my story. When he heard of the casualties, he looked shocked. There were a few moments of silence, then he quietly asked me who the men were and to write their families, which is the toughest job in the Navy and is traditionally done by the commanding officer involved in the action.

We were on our second drink when he said, "I have some good news! You and Monty have received promotions to lieutenant commander. However, the 51st doesn't rate two lieutenant commanders. Since Monty is a fine executive officer, I'm sorry to say that you'll have to be transferred. In fact, I've already requested it." He then handed me a set of shoulder boards displaying my new rank. "They aren't new, but you're welcome to them. Congratulations!" I was glad to receive the news and didn't at all mind leaving the 51st.

The next day was Sunday and I had some time off, so I drove over to the second Marine division's encampment on the other side of the island to lunch with Major Norwood Smith, the elder brother of a high school friend. I was amazed to see the Spartan way Marines lived, so different from us: minimum tents on the ground; spam, corned beef hash, and canned stew for almost every meal; no booze or beer; no officer's club; and nothing to do except drill, play cards, exercise, and fight with each other. Moreover, no Marine could leave camp. As far as I could see, the whole division was getting stir-crazy! Norwood said there was a rumor that Marines were treated this way in order to keep them mad and mean all the time.

The Navy was acknowledged by all services as having the best living conditions in the military, but the Seabees were the top of the Navy list except under combat conditions, which didn't occur often. We had good food including ice cream, prime meat, a variety of fresh and frozen food; had excellent clubs which were loaded with booze; had good movies; and lived in big airy tents with wooden floors. Almost every officer had a jeep and was free to go anywhere on the island as long as he'd gotten his work done. We thought the Marines lived like a bunch of corralled animals and acted that way. Maybe the rumor was right. If so, the treatment worked quite well. While I was in the Marine camp, I noticed an officer using a knife to carve a little inverted cone, like a crater, in the nose of each bullet he would use in his Colt 45 automatic pistol. I asked him why he was changing the bullets.

"It will stop a man who's running at you quicker than an issue bullet by putting a much bigger hole in him. It acts like a shot gun at close range," he said and then advised me to do the same. I asked him why the ammunition wasn't manufactured that way. He explained that it was forbidden by the Geneva Convention (an international agreement to reduce cruelty in war—what a laugh!). When I went back to camp, I spent the evening carving my ammunition. There was always a chance a Japanese hold-out would pop out of a cave somewhere.

One of the American Armed Forces' favorite pastimes was listening to Tokyo Rose, which we received on the radio in the officer's club. Tokyo Rose was a Japanese woman who broadcasted several hours every night from Tokyo to the American troops. (Today we'd call Tokyo Rose a disc jockey.) Her job was ostensibly to ruin the Americans' morale, but actually she had the opposite effect. She played the great, nostalgic American dance songs of the 1930s as well as the latest swing played by all the greats—Glen Miller, Tommy Dorsey, Benny Goodman, etc. In between records, she'd speak in perfect English, with a sweet, sultry, sexy voice. Supposedly she gave us the latest news and advice. Some of it was amazingly accurate.

"Hello, Fifth Marines on Saipan," she'd say. "Did your General McCabe tell you that you were going to attack Iwo Jima Tuesday morning at 0500? That's too bad. We will be waiting for you—and most of you will die. Of course, General McCabe doesn't care. He will stay on the ship in bed with one of the nurses. Has your wife or girlfriend written you lately? I hope so! It's been a long time hasn't it? It's a long time for her too, but she's not lonesome. There are lots of rich draft dodgers and service men with pull who are stationed back in the States. One of them is taking good care of her for you. I know he's living with her and wearing your clothes. Too bad for you, Marine. They're reading your letters in bed and laughing. You sucker!"

****

Jean and I tried to write each other every day, and thus she kept me updated on her pregnancy. She had decided to leave her job in Beverly Hills and go to live with her mother and father in Baton Rouge, Louisiana, until the baby was born. I encouraged her move because I didn't want her to be alone during this period. I was careful in my letters not to say anything that might worry her, although I'm sure she was worried anyway.

While still on Saipan, April 20, 1945, the news came that President Roosevelt had died. His death was a shock to everybody because he was a very much loved and admired Commander-In-Chief. In fact, I went so far as to go to a church memorial service for him—and going to church was unusual for me. On May 1, 1945 we got the wonderful news that Hitler was dead. That meant the war in Europe was about over, and soon the armed forces in the Pacific would get reinforcements from that theater. They would be needed since General MacArthur estimated that one million casualties would be incurred in conquering the Japanese homeland.

On May 8, even greater news was received. It was VE Day—Victory in Europe! It was only a matter of time now until the Japanese empire would crumble, and we could go home. Two days later on May 10, we received news that all the armed services were going to start releasing men to civilian status—how many hadn't been divulged. It would be done on a point system designed to favor length of service and time in combat. I was sure this meant I could get out soon and maybe miss the invasion of Japan. I had done my share of fighting and couldn't expect my good luck to last. You just can't win 'em all! I, along with thousands of others I'm sure, tried hard to find out more about the release, but were told to cool it. It would take many weeks to put the release into effect, and the American service men in Europe would be considered first. Their job was done.

On about May 30, 1945, I received a letter from Jean saying that a baby girl weighing almost nine pounds had been delivered on May 24 and that both she and the baby were healthy and happy. In our correspondence, Jean and I had agreed that should the baby be a girl, she would be named Sandra Sprague. And so she was. I was very glad Jean was with her mother and father in Louisiana. That night at the club we had a party to celebrate, and the drinks were on me.

****

Iwo Jima, the island that our planners figured to sew up in four days, took them twenty-four days. Seven thousand Marines were killed and 20,000 wounded. The Japanese casualties totaled 22,000 men, virtually all dead. However, before the war was over, 2,400 emergency landings were made by American B-29s on the island of Iwo Jima, so I guess the cost was worth it. The commander of the amphibian forces awarded me the Silver Star medal, but medals had ceased to mean much to me.

TWENTY-SEVEN

The Philippines, Samar, and Manicani Island

Around the first of June, I received my new orders. I was to report to the 30th Naval Construction Regiment stationed near the village of Guiuan on the Island of Samar, one of the central Philippine Islands. My new position would be Commanding Officer, Waterfront Construction and Dredging Detachment, Southern Philippines. It seemed to me that this would be fine duty. It meant I had an independent command—like a naval officer getting his own ship. It also meant that I probably wouldn't get pulled into the invasion of Japan, which was also just fine with me. I was to leave for my new posting at once.

Since I'd have to fly part of the way in a small airplane, I packed my footlocker with all my souvenirs, uniforms, letters from home, decorations, pictures, and the other belongings I'd acquired during this tour of duty until there was no room to spare. I shipped it by military freight to the 30th Construction Regiment, and it was the last I ever saw of it. I said good-bye to my buddies, all of whom were tired of Saipan, and considered me to be very lucky. I caught a ride in a Navy J2F-3 duck utility plane headed for Guam, where I spent forty-eight hours waiting for another plane going to my destination. While I was there, I stayed with an old friend of mine, Dan

Coykendall, who was commanding the 62nd Seabees. He entertained me very nicely and helped me get passage on an Army DC-3 Transport to the Naval air station on Samar, via the Palau Islands.

It was the most uncomfortable airplane ride I've ever taken. There were no seats in the plane and, except for the two pilots, I was the only passenger. Consequently, I sat on the floor in the back, traveling as baggage between spare machine parts. We finally landed at Peleliu, which had been in the middle of the war when I'd seen it last. Now it was almost an abandoned island with a desolate, burned landscape that looked like a Dali painting or a scene from Dante's Inferno. We refueled, stayed overnight in tents, then departed for Samar at dawn the next day.

The island of Samar lies 12 degrees north of the equator in approximately the center of the Philippine Archipelago. It's about the size of Hawaii, fairly mountainous, and covered with a dense tropical rain forest full of monkeys, parrots, crocodiles, and a great variety of strange indigenous animals. It's uncomfortably hot and humid all year-round—much like Guadalcanal, but even more swampy.

The southeast tip of the island had been cleared of growth and the swamp filled in. A huge American supply depot covering at least 200 acres had been established. On one edge of the depot a large naval air station had been built. On the side exposed to a protected harbor facing Leyte Gulf, large docks with ship cargo-handling equipment had been installed. Nearby was the native village of Guiuan, which supplied several hundred civilian workers for the supply base and girls for the American sailors.

When we landed at the air base, I phoned the 30th Construction Regiment located in the camp adjacent to the depot. Because I was a reporting lieutenant commander, they sent a jeep for me. I was assigned satisfactory temporary quarters, and that night dined with the regimental commander, a Captain Richie.

At dinner, the captain described my job. I was to take over the waterfront construction project on the island of Manicani, six miles away in the Leyte Gulf. The Navy was building a second large supply depot there. The 91st Construction Battalion was building the land facility and was camped on the island. They would give me logistical support for the 400 Seabees

The air field at Guiuan on the island of Samar.

assigned to the waterfront projects, but I would report directly to the regiment for military as well as construction duties. The captain also reminded me that I was in malaria country and so to begin taking atabrine daily, which fortunately I had already been doing. He believed malaria was particularly prevalent on Manicani because a number of cases had been reported there. In fact, the officer I was replacing had recently died of it.

The next day was spent with the operations officer who gave me a set of construction plans to study and took me to Manicani Island in a speed boat for an inspection tour and introductions. Manicani was about four miles in diameter and no more than a swampy rain forest. Why it had been selected for a supply depot site I'll never know. There must have been some very good reason because it was a very difficult place to live and work. The 91st Battalion was the saddest looking military outfit I'd ever seen. It had recently come to the Philippines from New Guinea, where it had been for a year. Its men and equipment were either worn out, rusted, or both.

The battalion had suffered many health casualties who had been hospitalized as the result of tropical illnesses such as malaria and amoebic dysentery. Some were never to return, and some who returned were not fully recovered and couldn't handle the strenuous work. There were no replacements; so the battalion had just dwindled. The morale of both officers and men was terrible.

The equipment was no better. It was rusted with holes big enough to climb through, and the bulldozers could hardly keep their tracks on. I thought to myself, *There was no way that this outfit is going to build that depot before the war is over.*

In contrast to the sad condition of the construction equipment, my waterfront equipment was a different story. It was relatively new and had a least a year to go before it would rust out even in this climate. The inventory consisted of twelve floating pile drivers that could handle steel sheet piles, several large bulldozers, three-tracked drag lines, two power shovels, five cranes, a flock of dump trucks, graders, boats, compressors, jeeps, a thirty-foot captain's gig for me, welding equipment, a machine shop, an underwater mapping boat with diving equipment, a blacksmith shop, miscellaneous tools and small equipment, and two big seagoing, deep-digging dredges: the *Louisiana*, a steam powered twelve-yard dragline rig, and the *Norfolk*, a thirty-six inch steam-powered turbine-driven hydraulic dredge. We even had plenty of spare parts and all the sheet piling necessary to build sea walls. My job was to build a harbor facility with along-side berths capable of docking at least five big freighters all at one time and of providing fast and efficient loading and unloading of military supplies and equipment which was to be used for the invasion of mainland Japan. I looked over the *Norfolk* and found the captain's quarters to be commodious and well equipped with a bed, chairs, ice box, shelves, phonograph, lockers, short wave radio, and a 180-degree view of the ocean. I decided to move in. I also decided to set up my own mess rather than eat at the 91st Officer's Club because being around these people would be depressing. The dredging operation, obviously, had been slowed down and become disorganized since the former captain's death.

I pointed this out to the operations officer and he agreed. He suggested that I move to the Norfolk the next day, take a couple of weeks to orient myself, then submit an operating plan with a tentative schedule. This made sense to me, and the next day I moved to my new quarters.

The following two weeks were spent meeting the crews, determining the capabilities of the equipment, and preparing a construction plan. It was easier preparing the plan than executing it, but I got the wheels moving by June 1. By then we were doing pretty well. Once a week, I took my boat over to regimental headquarters and discussed the progress and problems with the operations officer, Commander Brian O'Toole.

Along with other good advice, he warned me that the monsoon season was beginning, which meant weeks of strong winds from the southwest that would bring thunder storms and heavy rains daily. Additionally the odds of having a typhoon were fifty-fifty. This all meant that my floating equipment had to be very well anchored and shielded from heavy seas. Fortunately, I was working on the northeast side of the island; therefore, I had some protection.

Sure enough, by the end of July the weather deteriorated, and the whole island became a dark, dank, gloomy swamp. The 91st Battalion was submerged in a sea of mud and practically all work on the depot was shut down. Their tractors were stuck, and furthermore, almost half the crews were sick. I was able to keep working on a start-stop basis, but I couldn't keep the planned schedule.

I was for all practical purposes alone, without friends, and bored. Also, I was uncomfortable because I was always wet, had a fungus that ate away my fingernails and toenails, and a terrible rash on my feet. Gradually, I became more morose and depressed. The island was the tropics at its worst. It was like being a character in a Somerset Maugham or Joseph Conrad story. On August 8, 1945, I received word that on August 6 a great bomb, called an atom bomb, had been dropped on a Japanese city and wiped it out. This was great news. It looked like the beginning of the end. Then came August 15, Philippine time (August 14, U.S. time), when we got the news that President Truman had announced Japan's surrender. I got in my boat and took off for regimental headquarters. When I got there, all work had stopped and they were having parties everywhere. I found Captain Richie and asked him what we had to do to get orders home. He said he didn't know anything yet, but that when he did, he'd let me know right away. He wanted to go home too.

A couple of weeks later, the 91st got information about the Armed

Services personnel discharge policy and directions for application for it in the Philippines. It was simple: an applicant filled out a government form stating the number of points he or she had earned and submitted it to the local personnel officer for checking and forwarding to the Naval Construction Command of the Philippines in Manila, who ostensibly would then send back orders to discharge. The instructions said transport ships would soon be in Samar to pick up everybody. I needed fifty points and had one hundred or so. I went back to my regiment and found that Captain Richie, the executive officer, and most of the other officers had quit and gone to Manila for transport home. They forgot me.

Back at the 91st, I filled out three copies of the form and submitted one to regiment, one to the 91st, and kept one. At the end of the first week in September, a naval transport ship arrived at Samar and loaded the commanding officer and executive officer of the 91st and three-fourths of their men, plus virtually all of mine. Just before they left, I got orders appointing me commanding officer of the regiment, supposedly until someone decided what to do with the dredges and the remnants of the three battalions. Why I got the caretaker job I didn't know, but I found out very soon.

A courier delivered a letter to me from the Naval Construction Command in Manila stating that I would be visited by an Admiral Church, Civil Engineer Corp, USNR, and his party. They wished to inspect the waterfront equipment under my command. The party would arrive by plane at Guiuan Naval Air Station. I was to meet them and supply all transportation and stay with them until they left. This news sounded great since it probably meant I would be relieved in a few days.

The appointed day came and the inspection party arrived early in the morning. I met them at the air base and was surprised that the rear admiral was no more than forty years old. He was accompanied by a captain, two commanders, and three chief petty officers—all very friendly, congenial, and quite informal. I found out their schedule and arranged to have a good lunch and drinks sent out the *Norfolk* at noon.

The Admiral said all they wanted to see were the two dredges; so off we went across the six-mile channel in my admiral's gig. I explained that all work had been shut down since surrender because all the crews had left for home. They seemed to know this, and it became clear that they also knew a lot about me—at least they had read my service records. We spent four hours on the *Louisiana* and *Norfolk*, during which time all of the party proved to be knowledgeable concerning dredging. They asked all the right questions: fuel capacity and consumption, cubic yards of material that could be moved in an hour, seaworthiness, and availability of spare parts. Plus they asked several questions which seemed only to test my knowledge.

At a late lunch the Admiral told me that he was a reserve officer and before the war had been a vice president of the International Dredging Corporation out of New York. He was soon to be discharged and return to New York as president of the corporation. The other members of his staff would join his company as well. He expected my dredges would soon be declared surplus and International Dredging planned to buy them and the rest of the waterfront equipment. According to him it was already a sure thing—the corporation had friends in Washington as well as in the Navy who would see to it. He would then organize a Far East division of his company with headquarters in Manila, which would be staffed by the captain and the two commanders whom he had brought with him. The three chiefs would also return to the Philippines as civilians and look after the dredges themselves. They planned to negotiate a contract with the new Philippine government to clean up the harbors, which were full of sunken ships, and to rebuild the various waterfront shipping facilities which had been destroyed. Even the United States Navy would have a lot of work to do on their facilities in Manila Bay. Concurrently, the corporation would negotiate contracts to clean up the harbors in Hong Kong, Formosa, and Shanghai. Work for International Dredging in the Far East would last for years.

The Admiral wanted me to stay on in the Navy long enough to take the dredges to Manila, then get my discharge, and go to work for his Far East company. I explained that I was married and wanted the family together. He countered by saying that as soon as I had completed the above and signed up for the International Dredging Corp., he'd give me a salary of $1,000 a month plus a $1,000 bonus. After a few weeks on full pay in the

United States, I could return to Manila with Jean and the baby, all expenses paid, and live in a beautiful home with servants—like royalty. He also said that if I did well with the company, my future was unlimited. Since his family owned the company, he said he could guarantee his offer. He went on to say that if I would stay in the Philippines and look after the equipment until the sale to him was completed, he would additionally get me a spot promotion to full commander. The whole thing was unbelievable. It was the fattest offer I could imagine; in the States $400 a month was top pay for an engineer. On the other hand, who in hell wanted to live in the Far East? I thought of the white children brought up in Hawaii who always spoke with a pidgin English accent, no matter how well they were educated. Besides, I hated the Philippines. I told the Admiral I'd think about it and would let him know after I'd discussed it by mail with my wife. He looked disappointed but said he understood.

I realized then that as long as he was in the Navy, I'd be in Samar. He was the reason I wasn't on my way home now. He had to get that equipment to Manila and protect it until he could buy it, and even if he were successful, it might take months. It obviously was an inside deal that didn't sound very honest. But, I realized I was inexperienced and naive about such big business, and maybe everything was an inside deal. The Admiral told me that he would be leaving Manila in a week and that until he left he could handle cables back and forth to Jean for me. In any event, he had to know my answer soon.

It was 1400 and the sky was clouding up. Somebody reminded the party that in a couple of hours we'd be having afternoon thunder storms and it might be hard for them to fly home. Accordingly, we terminated the discussion, and I took them back to their waiting plane.

TWENTY-EIGHT

The War: The Final Chapter

AFTER I DROPPED OFF THE VISITORS AT THE SAMAR AIRPORT, I headed for the *Norfolk*. I wondered why I was more lonely and depressed than ever. Then it dawned on me that the reason was because control of my life was in the hands of others. I had to wait for somebody else to decide every move I made. I wasn't getting to make the moves I wanted, and furthermore, it didn't look like anyone even knew about me in this isolated, hellish place. I had no channels to go through. All the senior officers I knew who could do me any good had gone home. The war was over. I'd done what I had to do, and I wanted out. I was feeling sorry for myself and I knew it. I decided to go back to the *Norfolk*, sit down, and think through the whole situation. I'd do it the military way: make an estimate of the situation; establish objectives; identify the alternatives; and then develop a course of action.

As I roared across the channel in my boat, driven by my coxswain, there was a great flash followed by cracking thunder and the light rain turned to a downpour. The visibility became worse and worse, until the island of Manicani disappeared in the gloom. We slowed down and dinked along, following the compass home.

When I arrived, I checked the cook's larder to see how much frozen food we had and ordered a steak dinner served in my cabin. Then I went to my quarters, had a short shot of whiskey, took off my soaked clothes, and took a hot shower. I was still in mood indigo. The rain beat down harder than ever, and the wind and thunder made the ship sway and rattle. I was glad I wasn't in the small boat now. We'd be having a very hard time.

I started my analysis with the estimate. First, I was now a hard, tough man, both physically and mentally. I was much more a professional military type than a civilian engineer. I felt that I had forgotten everything I'd learned in school but had developed a few civilian skills. There was no doubt I'd have to rehabilitate myself considerably. I was cynical, feeling that the world had passed me by. I believed in luck—not God. The God I had learned about in the Episcopal church wouldn't have allowed war. Furthermore, I trusted no one very much except my family.

Secondly, during the last five years I'd worked in a very structured environment. Now, almost overnight, all discipline, organization, cooperation, and lines of communication had dissolved. Every one around me felt the way I did—the job was over. We were civilians at heart and wanted out, *now*, any way we could get out. No one cared about anyone else, and I was sure no one was looking after me. I was in a relatively isolated, inconvenient spot because the only functioning headquarters that could send me home now was in Manila, 350 flight miles away.

Thirdly, I had a special problem. Admiral Church was keeping me from getting orders home because he wanted me to look after the equipment he hoped to acquire. Although he said he was going home in a week, there still might be someone in headquarters who was looking after his interests— you never knew.

The objectives were easy. I wanted to go home, gather up Jean and the baby, and go back to graduate school—hopefully at Stanford. Then I wanted to settle down on the San Francisco peninsula. Afterwards, I wanted to own my own business, something that offered the chance of making plenty of money. The International Dredging job was absolutely out.

I had three alternatives. One was to leave things as they were, which put in the Navy's words were, "This man is presently indispensable to the U.S. Navy." The second was to go with Admiral Church; and the last was to fight my way out using the no holds barred technique—except to be sure that all the necessary legal papers were in order and filed. The third alternative, of course, was the only acceptable solution: get out at once without going AWOL.

I would have to improvise the course of action as I went along. I had to be bold, innovative, and ruthless. I had to use all my knowledge of military methods and procedures, and most important, I would take advantage of the shambles the personnel system was in. My ace in the hole would be that once Admiral Church and his staff had gone, nobody left in the hierarchy knew about me, or even cared.

The first course of action was to get rid of the only serious obligation that could really get me in trouble, which was $25,000 in United States currency that I had to accept from the 91st Construction Battalion when the disbursing officer left for discharge. The disbursing officers were supposed to transfer funds only to other disbursing officers, but there were no others around. Since I was the senior officer present and the regimental commanding officer, I was trapped. The money was locked in the *Norfolk's* safe, along with about $800 of my own that I had won playing dice. I had to get to Manila to get orders home anyway, so I would take the money there and turn it in to a disbursing officer. If I didn't do this, I could be accused of stealing it.

About 1800 my dinner arrived. I poured a before-dinner drink and turned on the phonograph. "A pretty girl is like a melody that haunts you night and day/Just like the strains of a haunting refrain." I was in the wrong mood. I flipped the record. "Love is like a cigarette..." I turned the phonograph off. The wind howled, the thunder boomed, and the ship shuddered. At that moment I knew that I must be the loneliest man in the world.

That night I slept poorly. I was restless and anxious. I got up early, flushed the cook out of bed, and had several cups of coffee with my usual spam and egg breakfast. We always had plenty of food around because I had the cook visit every newly-arrived Navy ship and bum it. When I was through eating, I went to what would have been the disbursing officer's cabin where the money was kept in the ship's safe. To my surprise, the cabin door was unlocked! I was sure I had locked it, just as I always did; and I had the only keys. My heart sank. I knew the door lock had been picked and that the money would be gone! When I looked, I found the whole safe had been stolen—all 200 pounds of it.

I went back and asked the cook where I could find Chief Storekeeper Grodin, who might shed some light on the problem since he seemed to always be around and knew what was going on. The cook said that he hadn't seen Grodin for over a week and that he was living ashore with a Filipino woman. Since I hadn't been around the dredge much lately, I hadn't noticed. I asked the cook if he knew of anything was missing.

He said, "Hell yes, Commander! Furniture, bedding, silverware, food, tools, fuel, vehicles—anything loose is being stolen and sold to the black market. Didn't you know?"

The fact was that I did know that Navy property was occasionally stolen to be sold or traded to the natives or perhaps to find its way to that phantom entity known as the black market. I knew this was the case whenever there were land-based troops occupying foreign lands; but nobody talked about it. I had read newspaper articles claiming that in Europe millions of dollars a day in supplies were stolen from the allied armies and sold through well-established channels to the desperately poor native population. Furthermore, high ranking American officials, as well as ordinary soldiers, were part of the black market conspiracy. However, I hadn't realized that we had a large active organization of this kind in the Philippines. I wasn't aware of it because it was very secret, and I had nothing to do with the military supply system.

It was of utmost importance that I get that money back because I was personally on the hook for it. I decided to find Chief Grodin. If he had anything to do with the black market, he wasn't going to tell me. However, I didn't know where else to start, and I thought he might inadvertently provide some leads.

It took three days to find Grodin. After a round-about search I found him living in a grass shack in the little settlement of Guiuan on Samar. A nice looking Filipino woman met me at the door. I gave her my name, and she disappeared for a minute or so. When she returned she said in pidgin English that Grodin wasn't there. It was obvious that he was there because a jeep from the 91st Seabees was parked outside. I brushed by her into the hut and found him sitting at a table with a bottle of whiskey. He jumped up when I came in. I cooled him off by assuring him that I didn't care whether he was AWOL or not, and explained that I just needed some information and hoped he would help me. After all, I reminded him, we had been friends. All he would say at first was that he knew nothing. For some reason, maybe he was flattered, he conversed with me for a couple of hours, loosening up more and more as he talked and drank. He, of course, made it clear that what he knew was only "scuttlebutt" that he'd heard. In the end with a little prodding, he told me what I wanted to know. Although he mentioned no names. There was a black market operating in the Philippines, and its activities had escalated, particularly since the recent ending of the war had left our military forces in such chaos.

On Manicani, Filipinos aided by American sailors were systematically pilfering the 91st Seabees and the dredging detachment. There was a local dump on the island where stolen goods were temporarily stored. The CPO wouldn't admit to knowing just where it was, but he thought "he knew," and indicated that it was across the island on south side. There was only one road crossing the island; so I figured I could find the dump.

I went back to the regimental headquarters and planned my first course of action. It was simple. First, I'd write out orders from regiment to the Commander, Philippine Islands Naval Construction Headquarters, ordering me to Manila for discharge and transportation home. Then I'd leave for Manila immediately after trying to recover the stolen money. I was certain that if anyone on Manicani knew I had that much cash, they'd kill me; so I couldn't stay around.

I wrote out the orders and signed them with Captain Richie's signature stamp, which he'd left in the desk when he evacuated, and put them in a courier's briefcase—the kind that locks and is chained to the wrist. I then went over to the air station to check the transportation. I told the operations officer that I was a courier who would be needing a ride the next day. He said there were no regularly scheduled flights and that I'd just have to wait until some airplane came through headed for Manila. As we talked, I noticed three Navy SNJs sitting on the ramp. If necessary, I could talk my way into getting one of those to fly myself to Manila.

That night I stayed on the *Norfolk* at Manicani. Very early the next morning after a couple of cups of coffee, I checked to see that my Colt 45 automatic was fully loaded with the cartridges I had modified, put six extra loaded magazines in my ammunition belt pouch, then set out in my jeep along the jungle road that bisected the island. In about a half an hour, I reached the beach on the southern side of the island where the road turned right and continued across the headland which formed one side of a sheltered cove.

Fronting on the cove was a clearing of maybe ten acres with a double length barracks-type quonset hut standing in front and several native huts in the rear. Except for the quonset, the place looked like a native village, with chickens running around and clothes hanging on lines. Near the beach stood several jeeps and a stack of gasoline drums, all probably waiting to be loaded on a landing boat and delivered to the black market. In front of the huts a couple of women stood and talked. Other than the women and chickens, there was no activity.

I nervously checked my gun again. It was cocked with the safety on. Being a left-handed shooter and wearing a government issued holster that hung on the right side of my waist made it very clumsy for me to pull a gun in a hurry; therefore, I stuck it in my belt. I headed for the quonset hut. The adrenaline was running, the intensity of a combat high coming on with its attendant cold sweat and the pounding heart. Everything looked bigger than life.

I opened the door. Behind a desk located in front of a wooden bulkhead sat a husky Filipino, my age or a little older, reading a newspaper. He looked up, startled, and said in good English, "What the hell do you want?"

Automatically I scanned the room. There were dozens of U.S. carbines stacked against the wall, boxes of ammunition, a couple of sub-machine guns, three or four gasoline jerry cans, a pile of miscellaneous boxes, and there in the corner was the safe with the name USS *NORFOLK* painted on its front. "Who the hell are you?" This time, the Filipino shouted. I told him who I was and what I wanted. "Are you trying to shake me down, Commander?"

"No. It's just as I said. All I want is the safe and its contents, or what were the contents," I said and put my hand on my gun.

"You can go to hell," he sneered.

I pulled my gun and snapped off the safety. He sat down and said in a most conciliatory tone, "Let's be reasonable. You're out of your territory and out of your mind. Come on now, I'll give you a nice girl and a bottle, and you can have some fun. We'll forget this."

I watched his right hand slowly move over to the desk drawer and pull it open. I could see the tortoise shell butt of a hand gun. I knew then that he didn't think I'd shoot. He had misinterpreted my trembling hand for fright, and I knew he'd shoot me no matter what I did now. However, I had no plans to die. I pointed my gun at his face and squeezed. The blast of that .45 inside that tin building is indescribable. Outside, there was a cacophony of sound—screaming women, squawking chickens, chattering monkeys. The Filipino fell over backwards in his chair, headless.

The whole episode hadn't taken three minutes. I walked over to the combination safe and opened it with fumbling, trembling fingers. Everything was there. The safe was too heavy for me to carry, so I stuffed the contents without taking the time to count the money into a couple of cardboard boxes and put them in my jeep. I started the engine and then hurried back to the quonset hut where I unscrewed the tops from three of the jerry cans of gasoline and kicked them over on the floor. As I went out the door, I tossed a hand grenade on the spreading gasoline and ran for the jeep and took off. The quonset hut burst into flames with a roar. Now there was nothing to explain—just a memory!

When I got back to the *Norfolk,* I packed my belongings in a sea bag and counted the money. It was all there, including the receipt, and my $800. Then alone in my speedboat, I headed for the mainland and regimental headquarters. When I looked back at Manicani, I could see smoke still rising from the burning quonset hut.

As usual, it had started to rain and the afternoon thunder storms were forming. Accordingly, I decided it was too dangerous to try to fly out that night. At headquarters, I packed the government's money in the leather courier case and put it in the regiment's safe. Early the next morning, I took the money and went to the airport operations officer, flaunting the courier case chained to my arm and demanded transportation to Manila.

The only officer on duty was an ensign. He said there was no traffic scheduled that day but that something might come along. Then, I demanded one of the SNJs. He said okay but that he'd have to see my log, ID. card, and my pilot's license, which I wasn't carrying. Then I sternly demanded his name rank and serial number. That did it!

"Okay. Hell take the plane you want, Commander. You'll have to fill it up with gas, yourself. Sir, I'm not even going to log it. Just go," he said. The 350 mile flight to Manila that morning was a relaxing, enjoyable event. The clouds were scattered, the sea was a deep navy blue, and the old thrill of flying returned to me. I hadn't realized how very much I'd missed it. I flew at about 3,000 feet, followed the west coast of Samar in a northwesterly direction to Luzon, then continued over the Sibuyan Sea, crossing hundreds of little islands. After about two and a half hours, I passed over Manila. I wanted to land as close as I could to Cavite Naval Shipyard. I circled Cavite until I spotted an active field and then landed.

I parked the plane and found a ride to the Cavite Navy Yard Officer's quarters. I showed them my I.D. card and orders and got a room immediately. After lunch, I found out where the yard disbursing officer was and visited him with my courier's case full of money. I asked for the senior officer present and was received by a captain, Supply Corps. I explained the situation, showed him my receipt, I.D., orders, and counted out the $25,000. He thanked me, took the money, and gave me a receipt for it. What a relief, but what an ordeal it was to get it. I felt like a great load was suddenly lifted from my shoulders. I'd hate to be a disbursing officer.

Now I had to figure out how I was going to ship out. First, I had to get a clearance from the commanding officer, Naval Construction Headquarters, Philippine Islands. The orders I carried really only got me to Manila. My first step was to ascertain that Admiral Church and staff had left, which I did by simply going to the receptionist and asking for Church or one of his staff. He was gone.

The next step, actually getting the clearance for a discharge was more delicate. I found the chief yeoman who prepared all the papers for the Admiral's signature. I feared that he might possibly know what was going on, recognize that Captain Richie who had signed my orders wasn't around, and realize that something was fishy. I also knew he really didn't care. I would have to give the chief an incentive. I got an appointment with him quite easily. When I said that I needed orders, he informed my that there were at least a hundred people ahead of me and that I'd have to wait. I asked him if a hundred dollars, American, would help. He said that a hundred and fifty dollars would get the orders the next day and that I should come back in the morning. The next morning, I got the orders. The next hurdle was to get a ship. There was one loading that day. Again, when I approached the transport command, I got the same answer as before, except this one only cost me a hundred dollars. The next day I sailed for home.

The trip home was pleasant and lucky. I won a thousand dollars, plus or minus, playing 4-5-6, a game that vaguely resembled craps and was played with three dice. The person shooting the dice couldn't pull money out of the pot between throws, and everybody had to add to the kitty on each throw. It was a crazy game with big pots and big winners.

****

We landed in Seattle somewhere around the end of October. From Seattle, I went to Chicago on the Great Northern Railroad; and from there, to Baton Rouge, Louisiana, on the Baltimore and Ohio Railroad. Baton Rouge was home because Jean and Sandra were there. They met me at the station. I gave Sandra a great big kiss. When I kissed Jean, I squeezed her so hard I broke her rib.

Epilogue

S OON AFTER CHARLES RETURNED TO THE US, he, Jean, and baby Sandra moved to the San Francisco Bay Area. Charles returned to Stanford University and obtained masters degrees in engineering and economics.

Throughout his life, Charles continued to embody the Seabee "can do" motto. He built two successful businesses. The first he started in 1950, soon after leaving Stanford. It was a sanitary engineering firm that designed and constructed water and sewage treatment plants for small cities in central and northern California, Nevada, and Mexico. The second was a construction and real estate development company that he started in 1969 in the heart of what would become the Silicon Valley. Over the next twenty years, he became a major developer of R & D and office buildings in the area.

Charles spent thirty years in the Naval Reserves, retiring as a Captain in the mid-1970s. His love of flying continued throughout his life. As soon as he could afford it, he bought an airplane that he used for traveling to the small California towns and to Mexico where he did his engineering work. In later years, he always had a plane for leisure travel and for simply flying on sunny California afternoons.

Charles and Jean had four children—Sandra and three boys, Birk, Greg, and Jett—and ten grandchildren. Charles passed away in 2001 at the age of 83. He was among loved ones in the house he and Jean built in Los Altos Hills, CA. Jean lived another twelve years.